In My Life, So Far…

Georgiana Steele-Waller

ISBN 978-0-6151-4585-3

Dedication:

To all the people whose paths crossed with mine over the years, creating memories, both good and bad. And to my husband, Gordon, my inspiration and strength, through the good times and the bad, it taught me a lot.
And to Sun, the best horse in the world.

Chapter 1

If I knew where it all began I would begin at the beginning. Oh, there is the obvious beginning, the 27th December 1949, 1:15 am at Kings College Hospital in London, England, but that is the beginning of life only, not the beginning of the LIFE, as in life-style, I suppose.

Being born rather late in my parents lives, for the times, might have had something to do with my inclusion into their world of social activities.

My father, Geoffrey Steele, an ex-British army officer, actually Cavalry, the First Royal Dragoons escaped the regular army after the war by becoming ill with bronchial fibrosis and no longer fit to partake of active military service. He was quite pleased with that decision as his entire family (the male side anyway) had practically been wiped out from being in the regular army, so he could now proceed with his real love of acting. He had begun his life in a tin-roofed shed in Potchefstroom, So. Africa on June 27th, 1914. His father George Frederick Steele had been in charge of his regiment (The Royals) and when his mother Muriel had traveled down there to visit he was born there. He only spent the first 10 weeks of his life in So. Africa before returning with his mother to England and soon after came the news that his father had been killed in Ypes, Northern France during a battle in the First World War in 1915. This was when my father was only 10 months old. Later on his mother re-married Alistair Sinclair Campbell who took them all to his tea plantation in Shanghai, China in the 1920's, where dad attended the Cathedral School in Shanghai.

Then back to England where all seemed idyllic till "Jimmy" as his step-father was called died as a result of being mustard-gassed in WWI. So, two people close to him had been killed off by the British Army (and the Germans) as he saw it, and though he did his duty and went to St. Andrew's, Eton and Sandhurst, where he was a champion at the high-hurdles, destined for the 1936 Olympics, only to have those hopes dashed by having to go and join his regiment in India and Egypt. Those were the Olympics that Hitler refused to shake hands with Jesse

1

Owens and all hell broke loose a few years later with the onset of WWII.

My father entered the world he loved, that of the theatre and early days of television. He acted in and produced the very first play ever televised on electronic television in the world. A play called "Marigold" televised from the Alexandria Palace in London in 1936.

He later worked with Cecil Madden at the BBC and is in a book called *'Adventures In Vision'* all about the early days of television.

He soon traveled to America with his mother and took up residence at the Beverly Wilshire Hotel, from there he pursued a career in Hollywood and did many films such as Casablanca, Terror By Night and so forth.

My mother was born in Cedarhurst, Long Island, New York on September 26th, 1911.

Her father, Joseph A. Shay was a barrister (lawyer) who worked on some famous criminal cases such as the Becker trials in the 20's and 30's. Both her mother and father had come from Syracuse, New York and before that the families had been from Germany and had fled to avoid their sons from being drafted into Bismarck's army.

A socialite in New York and Palm Beach, Florida, my mother was educated in France and Switzerland. She had come back to New York and married and divorced twice to two men of the F. Scott Fitzgerald era. Her first marriage to Thomas Frances Murphy ended after only six months and the second to Winthrop Gardner Jr. of Gardner's Island, New York ended some scant nine months later when he ran off with the Olympic Ice Skater and actress Sonja Hennie.

My mother headed for California after that and got into pictures, under contract to Cecil B. Demille in the 30s doing such films as *'Balalika'* with Nelson Eddy and *'The Women'* with Joan Crawford for George Cukor among many others, some 23 in those early days of her career.

My parents met around the swimming pool at the Beverly Wilshire Hotel in August of 1941. Though they had apparently seen each other at various parties around Hollywood, especially at the home of Maggie Roach, who my dad had dated and who was also a friend of my mothers.

Maggie was the daughter of Hal Roach, producer of the *Our Gang* Comedies.

2

Four days after they met again they went off to Las Vegas and got married in the jail with two drunks in the drunk tank as witnesses!

My parents, Geoffrey & Mildred Steele

With the war well underway in Europe all it took was the bombing of Pearl Harbor on December 7th 1941 and my father and mother went back to England so that my dad could rejoin his regiment. The whole thing taking longer than usual as the Cavalry had not been mechanized as yet so the Army put them up at the Savoy Hotel in London.

As my father had a background in show-business he was sent up to Barnard Castle in Yorkshire to make training films for the army and never went over the Channel.

This was a blessing as his entire regiment was wiped out at Bengazzi in North Africa.

After the war, as I said he was down to 142 lbs. which on a 6'1 1/2" frame was a little too light with this bronchial fibrosis and he was deemed permanently unfit for any form of military service. After trying to make a living in the theatre and the newly established television industry in post-war Britain, and after my birth at the end of 1949 they decided to try America again.

The Korean War was going by late 1950 and there were openings everywhere to be filled till the soldiers came home again. My father obtained a position at NBC in New York as a UPM (Unit Production Manager) and we moved to the Hotel Versailles on 57th and Madison, then to the new Fresh Meadows in Flushing and finally out to Atlantic Beach, Long Island, a house on the beach. Then onto Hollywood in 1954.

I guess it was the parties in Hollywood and the then burgeoning San Fernando Valley where we lived eventually after a few apartments in West Hollywood like The Gables on Fountain. Some of my earliest memories of the fun life had to offer was centered around these parties.

The planning and organizing, the preparations, the good mood everyone was usually in getting ready for and during these events.

Then there were the parties themselves. These elaborate affairs left over from a bygone era. In the fifties they were still a left over from the 30s and 40s, just as today we tend to recreate our glory days of the 60s and 70s.

There were the monthly parties held by the Astrologer Carroll Righter. He would have a party each month for each astrological sign, usually with the symbol for that sign somewhere on the premises. For instance, a ram on the lawn for Aries, a bull for Taurus, twins for Gemini, and so on. Even a lion for Leo!

He would introduce you around by sign, not name. "Mr. Moon Child" (never Cancer),"I'd like you to meet Miss Capricorn," and so on.

But, I digress, as I probably will do continuously throughout this narrative.

The people also, I know they had a lot to do with forming my ideas of what was fun. To a small child of 4, 5, or 6 years of age having the likes of Cary Grant, John Carradine, C. Aubry Smith, Boris Karloff, Jon Hall, Maxwell Reed, to name but a few, be the uncles that always become of your parents friends changes your level of reality, and normality to say the least.

To a young mind, seeing *"Frankenstein"* at night on TV and then seeing Boris Karloff at a Halloween party in the bar-room my father built in part of our barn/garage in the then very rural Van Nuys, well you can imagine a slight blurring of the lines of reality.

I spent many a week-end at the Carradines' ranch in Calabassas, now an historical monument I understand. John Carradine was married at that time to Sonia, and my parents home seemed to always be a refuge for one or the other of them when they had an argument going on in Calabassas.

I had a few horseback riding adventures at the ranch. Like when the horse I was on, at about age eight, suddenly took off, my dad jumped on Sonia's grey Arab stallion, Snowy, bare-back, and took chase. My horse had come to rest by the time he had caught up, on the other side of what is now the Ventura freeway. Thank goodness it was only a seldom traveled highway back then!

Dad, Mum and myself around 1957.

I must add here the continuing love for horses I have always had. My father had been in the British Cavalry, the First Royal Dragoons, now the Blues and Royals.

I was placed on a pony at 15 months of age riding at 18 months, at about 10, with reins tied and arms crossed I was set over six 3 foot jumps. I still ride my beautiful Tennessee Walking Horse stallion Sun's Dark Chance almost daily, as I have since I got him in 1985.

I guess all of this did a good deal towards making all the mundane things, like school, not quite for me. Oh, the learning was interesting, the discipline, regimentation and boring stuff that restricted me to their pace instead of mine, was not at all my cup of tea. I don't think I ever really liked school, though I can remember liking the process of learning, the trouble with that was when I was interested in something and wanted to carry it further the powers that were the teachers went onto some other subject that didn't quite capture my interest.

This also helped to alienate me from most of my contemporaries, it was much more fun to crawl all over 'Jungle Jim' AKA Jon Hall at a cocktail party, or to ride on the back of Maxwell Reeds' motorcycle, a'la "*The Wild Ones*" than to play with kids my own age outside of the social scene I found myself in with my family. Other children always seemed to have too many time limits and restrictions put on them anyway.

I was a shy child around other kids, with a sophistication far beyond my years. It was hard for me to communicate with them on a kids level. But with the friends of my parents I blossomed. I don't know that this was always such a good thing, but it hasn't caused any deep-seated traumas I can think of, not in the past 50 odd years anyway, and the memories are far richer than any playground adversities I may have had.

I can envision at the age of 6 or 7 after leaving a party in Bel Air one night with my parents with a contingent of their British Colony friends in tow, to party on at our house in the Valley.

A dear friend of my father's and fellow English actor, Ronald Long, much the worse for drink, insisted we stop at a market on the way, to buy a duck. The only duck in existence was frozen. When we got home it was still frozen to the density of a brick. But Ronnie persisted in bar-b-quing it anyway, all the while reciting the Witches' [Weird Sisters] speech from "Macbeth" ("toil, toil trouble and boil...")

These kind of things were the stuff my memories were made of. I can't recall much of anything in my day-to-day life with the neighbourhood children, or at school. (By the way the duck was nothing but blackened bones in the end)

At least my parents were considerate enough to let me stay up into the wee hours so as I could join in the merriment.

Looking back into my memories it seems now that my life then was full of experiences like that. Of course life wasn't always a party, but it's pretty much all I can remember with any clarity. The absurd and silly stuff especially. Lots of fun for a child growing up in a world of adults who never grew up, who never wanted to grow up. Not really very practical though.

Chapter 2

Before I left school, I left school. Not too interested in things scholastic taught at random, and to me, for no apparent reason at the time, and not thinking toward the future either, I embarked on a foray into the world of fashion modeling.

Thanks to a God-mother in the fashion business I got signed with an agent, Fran O'Brien. This was in 1963 or so and I was about 13. This was another nudge into a world separate from the ordinary, so I liked it just fine. I did quite well too, and in no time I had graced the pages of *Teen* and *Seventeen* magazines, among other publications of the same ilk. I then moved on to the Nina Blanchard Agency which was then located at the corner of Hollywood Blvd. and Highland Ave. which is now the site of the new Kodak Theatre built to house the Academy Award presentations. Though models didn't demand the same salaries they do today, for the early sixties it was better than a paper route, or babysitting.

At about the same age, 13 or 14 I also dabbled in the movie or rather the television industry through yet another contact of my mothers'. The casting director, Walter Donnegar was a friend of hers and happened to be casting the TV series *Peyton Place*. I resembled the young Mia Farrow and for a spell was her stand-in/photo double. Going to school on the set on the Twentieth Century Fox lot, walking through the set for the *Batman* series everyday wasn't anything special after a while. I can recall Frank Sinatra showing up for the 17th birthday of his then-to-be future wife Mia. Nothing too special there either. When Mia left the series Walter told my parents I could be up for taking over the role. Something I stupidly refused flat out to even consider. Oh, the follies of youth!

ise That Refreshes---Modeli

the first of four articles on teen-ning.

BY JULIE BYRNE
Times Staff Writer

ge models may be sisters under
with high school and college
the kinship stops right there in
ses. Because the models have
how, and done the necessary
ck, to solve their skin, hair and
oblems.
very girl wants to be a model,
an profit by studying the fresh-
hiny-haired models with their
oise and confidence,
makes them so attractive? As
ung models represent the "in"
youth, we interviewed a num-
em to find out how they really
their stock in trade—fresh good

ure articles these girls will open
bag of beauty tricks and advice
in, hair and body care.
thing is quickly apparent. If
ss is next to Godliness, it is one
er to "modeliness." These girls
r by soap and water,
scrubbed, well-brushed look is a
l weapon in getting television
cials, the highest paying job a
an get," says the head of one
gency.
reciate your own age," says an-

s potent advice,
g girls have a natural radiance
y older woman would give up
ks and diamonds to attain.
the most of youth. It won't last
and there's plenty of time for
make-up and hairdos when the
ll around.
r model interviewed stressed
d hair cleanliness, balanced diet
nness and bright-eyed health.
old make-up to a minimum and
ate in sports or take dancing for
-ordination.
selected three young models,
Wagner, Candy Wells and
nna Steele, who will share their
secrets. Like their student sis-
ey are teen-agers and are still in

OFF TO WORK—Teen-age models Georgianna Steele, Lindsay Wagner and Candy Wells, from left, combine school and work. They agree that shining make-up and swinging steps can be a girl
Times photo by Mar

L.A. Times series on modeling. Me, Lindsay Wagner, and Candy Wells.

Now music was a force to be reckoned with in the sixties. Needless to say, as it has been said, but it did a lot in the shaping of the fashion and art, and the total lifestyle of our generation, and of the generations to come.

Along about this time in the scheme of things, the Beatles first hit these shores in February of 1964, and all hell broke loose. The albums were bought, the magazines were bought, [usually in triplicate so as to be able to stick both sides up on my wall and still have a copy to read.]

This kind of thing was in no way peculiar just to me. It was indeed a universal mania.

By August 1964 with an appearance on the West Coast of the Beatles looming on the horizon, I just couldn't wait for the Los Angeles at the Hollywood Bowl performance and managed to convince my parents that it was imperative that I travel to Las Vegas for the performance at the Convention Center on the 23rd August 1964. My mother must have figured it would be a good chance to go to Vegas or something as my dad got me the ticket for the show (I believe it cost all of $3.98 or some such impossible price!)

So, off we went by train from Union Station in downtown L.A. on the now vanished Desert Wind train service, one sultry August morning in that long ago land of black and white.

Two friends from school also convinced their parents this was a necessary experience and that my mother was a fit chaperon, so Andrea Shanker and Arlene Kuritsky made it four.

We stayed at the Sahara Hotel on the Strip, and as the fates would have it, so did the Beatles.

One afternoon while lying around the pool, I had been chatting to a girl, who as it turned out was either the secretary or assistant to either (again memory is fuzzy) Brian Epstein, the Beatles manager, or Neil Aspinall, their tour manager.

Being that I was British, one thing led to another, and she suggested I come up to their floor while she changed and meet someone or other I believe it was Neil Aspinall. They both conferred and it was again suggested further that I come to the Convention Center and meet the lads before the show.

So began my inadvertently never really needing tickets for shows, whether I had them or not.

Dressed in my new black lace cocktail dress, black stiletto heels and long black gloves (hey, it was Vegas in 1964), I stood outside the dressing room door at the Las Vegas Convention Center, and when Pat Boone and his little daughter Debbie came out from their meeting with the Beatles, I was escorted in.

1964

There they were, just sitting around like young boys anywhere, which of course they were, with a really good gig, eating burgers and malts and French fries. So I sat too. They joked around and sang snippets of this and that, not Beatle songs, *"Walkin' the Dog"* was running through someone's mind as I recall, as they were singing as though singing along to the radio. Basically, we just hung out. When it was time to go on-stage, I stood in the wings, just to the right of the raised stage, and even from there had trouble hearing through the endless screams. I loved every minute. My new friends were up there.

I was carried along in the excitement, not only that, I was included in it, a part of it.

In the mad rush to get out of the venue in one piece, I was swept into the Brinks armoured truck that was being used for transportation a lot for groups back then, and off back to the Sahara. Here they were being taken by freight elevator in the kitchen, and Ringo handed me a key to go on and open up the room, I think he meant for me to hand it to Mal Evans, but I felt part of the road crew at that moment and Mal, dear Mal, played along.

Mal told me this years later in L.A., it was shortly before he was tragically shot to death by the L.A.P D.

Mal had been with the Beatles since the beginning practically, he is the one who keeps popping up in the *Help* movie asking "White Cliffs of Dover?"

Mal had gotten a bit out of it and there was some sort of standoff situation where he was shot by the police. Enough said.

No pretentious big suites for the most popular band of all time. Just a floor of regular rooms, two twin beds and a T.V., though there was a suite at the end of the hall.

As soon as George Harrison sighted me again, which wasn't difficult in a room of that size, he got me a drink in a tall glass which consisted of 2/3rds Scotch and 1/3rd Coke. He offered me a Marlboro (hey, I'd smoked in the bathroom of Milliken Jr. High), and I was on my way.

Speaking of smoking in the Milliken bathroom, that's how I met my best friend, Heidi Friars. A bunch of us girls were passing a cigarette around, and someone yelled that a teacher was coming our way and they all ran. I tossed the butt in the trash can and it started to smolder. No teacher, just Heidi comes walking in. "Oh cool! A fire" says she, piling more paper towels in the trash. Someone told on us and we were suspended for a week, so we started hanging out together.

Heidi was a Class A Beatle fanatic as well. Poor Heidi, her mom made her go to summer camp instead of being able to come to Las Vegas with us.

So, back to Vegas. I was told I could invite one of my friends to the party. Never a good decision maker, I left it up to Andrea, AKA Andie, and Arlene to sort it out. It was Arlene who prevailed. Andie managed to get both of the Righteous Brothers into the bungalow my mum and I were sharing and my mother says that when she walked in and found them all together she took great pleasure in giving Andrea a resounding slap. I don't think they were doing anything at all, really, but we were all 14 years old and she was responsible for us. Something that came back on her anyway when Arlenes' family found out their daughter had spent the night in a suite of rooms occupied by the Beatles, they promptly sued, I think they got $5,000. It was so embarassing. Fortunately, the world wasn't as litigation happy as it has since become, nor so politically correct, and the word "groupie" was yet to become part of the English, or shall I say, world language. It was still fans then. But I get ahead of myself.

The party was under way. Lots of memories connected with this one. Snippets include: Going into the bathroom and John Lennon kicking the door open and chasing me around and through the shower/bath, never catching me. But I don' t think that was really his intention anyway. Paul McCartney left early with Jackie DeShannon, who along with the Ronnettes was also on the bill that tour. Going down the hall with George Harrison to the only actual suite I saw, and making out on the white sectional sofa, where all I got was a hickey, which I tried to keep with tangee lipstick long after it had faded, ah, youth! John came bounding in through a connecting room dressed only in red and white polka-dot boxer shorts. George took a Polaroid of this, which I had until I foolishly sent it to a pen pal in Gateshead, County Durham, England named Lorna Douglas, who, needless to say neither sent it back nor I don't think ever wrote again.

Meanwhile, back in the main party room, my mum phoned up periodically, as the hour got later, only to be told by Derek Taylor, the Beatles publicist Mal Evans, Neil Aspinall and all & sundry that I was safe as houses a very northern English term for being , well safe. I recall Ringo also saying this to her once, he was brushing my hair at the time. We were all very chummy, and very young.

The upshot of all this phoning was that my mum said I should really come back downstairs as we were leaving to go back to L.A. in the morning. "Oh, we're going to L.A., why don't you come along with us?" It was decided it would be O.K., little did she know, nor I, perhaps not even whoever in the band suggested it, that they were not going directly to L.A. from Vegas, but rather via Seattle and Vancouver!

I soon succumbed to the drink and the hour and lay across one of the twin beds and passed out. I recall that was the first time I had that feeling of the room spinning when I closed my eyes, but being too out of it to keep them open. When I did open them, well past the dawn, the first thing that greeted my eyes was a sound asleep John Lennon lying across the same bed, what a trip. And what an innocent trip. We were the innocents then. It was only the foul-minded sheriff of Las Vegas having found that there had been underage girls in rooms of those 'long-haired English guys', said nastily to my mother, "I hope you don't have any little Beatles!" This probably gave the Kuritsky's the idea that they could sue. But nothing untoward happened. We were cool. A good time was had by all, and the tour continued. My mother trusted me to be with them, and so she should.

The stage was set, so to speak. After that summer I went back to school. High school this time. I attended Ulysses S. Grant High School in Van Nuys. But not for long. Between the modeling and the 60s I just couldn't settle down. There was something out there and I didn't want to miss a minute of it.

Through lack of interest, and the clothes I chose to wear, it was decided I should discontinue my sojourn at Grant after just one semester. No problem. My friend Heidi had already dropped out due to pregnancy. Her mum should have let her come to Las Vegas.

This brings another little side trip into the halls of infamy. The father of Heidi's baby was "Bummer" Bob Beausolais, who went to prison at Atasquadero for killing musician Gary Hindeman, orchestrated by none other than Charlie Manson.. I'm told he went to Atasquadero as criminally insane. This preceded the Tate/LaBianca killings that were to make the rest of the Manson family famous, or infamous. I've recently heard that he has just been paroled. Enough of this for now.

It was now about 1965 and off I went with my new career of modeling, going to Hollywood Professional School only four hours a day either mornings or in the afternoon, depending on when I might have work, I could dress more avant guard, and it put me in Hollywood.

Around this time, I was hired to do a tour of fashion shows for the Broadway Department Stores in Southern California. They were previewing a new line of clothes from British designer Caroline Charles. The new style was going to be thoroughly modern, and hip and innovative. They had a live rock 'n' roll band play as the models danced down the runway. This was to show how well the clothes moved.

The band consisted of some local guys who called themselves The Bees, and I am still good friends with one of its' members, John York, who later played with such people as Johnny Rivers, the Sir Douglas Quintet, and the Byrds.

Caroline Charles, seated, London's new top designer of young fashions, checks modes worn by Georgiana Steele, left, and Susie Mette, before Saturday's show at Broadway Grossmont store.

Mode Show's A 'Rocker' – And The Clothes A Smash!

We danced all over the place. It was on the last of these shows that I took my first plane ride, to San Diego and back. John said, as we landed in L.A., that the tour was over, so the no fraternization rule was also over, and he leaned over and kissed me.

It was the beginning of a beautiful friendship.

15

John had moved to L.A. from New York with two friends: Marc B. Ray and Russell Gilbert.

They rented a modern 'A' frame house on Ridpath in Laurel Canyon. I used to go over after school, sometimes I just skipped the school part and went straight there.

Now Marc and Russell were older that John, and John was three or four years older than I. Marc kept pretty much to himself and didn't join in the activities of the rest of the household, which was cool. No interference either, we just went our own ways.

Russell was a Capricorn and an experimenter. We got along great, he was a really sweet individual and very caring. He died years ago, in mysterious circumstances involving the government, or so I've heard. He thought he looked like the drawing of Christ in Kahlil Gibrans' book *The Prophet* and he did.

I had been smoking pot for a while by this time. This all began when a friend, Cheryl Gross, who was older and had a license, borrowed my mothers car and took Heidi and I out for the evening. What she did was drop us off at a friend of hers' Steve Venet's house and took off to do her own thing. Cheryl is still around, she changed her name to Iris and got married. She and another friend from school, Sheri Crawford and I still are in touch quite regularly. Anyway, Heidi and I were just sitting around with this guy and listening to Bob Dylan's *"Bringing It All back Home"* album, smoking our first joint, it was a very cool scene for starting in this direction. Acid was still fairly new to the populace in general. I had been given it experimentally by the psychiatrists at the UCLA Neuro-Psychiatric Hospital.

My parents had sent me to see a child psychologist there. I don't think I had anything more than growing pains, neither did they, but my parents wanted to be sure, they didn't really know anything about raising kids, or teens, as they didn't have any friends with kids really, and going to a shrink was trendy at the time.

So, I went and discussed my pre and post pubescent problems with Dr. Gay. I recall I didn't really care for him very much, and neither did my father.

The up-shot was that through testing I turned out to be so well-balanced emotionally that it was suggested I be included in a testing program they were doing there with a new experimental drug called

Lysergic Acid Diethylidamine. LSD being the more common diminutive. So I was given four doses, or trips,over a length of time that year, and had all sorts of clinical studies done, looking at ink blots and that kind of stuff. They were trying LSD on schizophrenics at the time, and also for treating forms of addiction like heroin and alcoholism.

Anyway this was my first introduction to Acid. I was about 15.

Chapter 3

Being an experimenter and searcher, Russell Gilbert was about the only other person I knew at that time who had taken Acid as well.

I actually hadn't thought of myself as having taken Acid either. It just turned out to be the same drug, but not the same trip at all.

Russell and I decided to take a trip. It was a big plan.

He was going to take me riding on his motorcycle down Sunset Blvd, and to the beach to the Self-Realization Center. We even had the day all picked out. Unfortunately it rained, so we took it at the A-frame house on Ridpath instead.

I took a lot of psychedelics over the ensuing years, but this particular trip stands out as the singularly most perfect psychedelic experience of them all.

My friend, and I guess sort of a pen pal in Liverpool, Chris Skelton, was by then in the habit of sending me the new Beatles albums as they were released in Britain. They always pre-released the release date in America.

As luck would have it, I had just received the new *Revolver* album. Russell also possessed the latest in stereophonic technology so I took it over to the house that day, and over fifteen hours or so listened to it on stereo headphones.

But I did other stuff too.

Some of the lasting impressions I have are going outside into the still and wet night in the Canyon looking up into the green, purple, and silver starlit sky, and observing raindrops that made everything sparkle like they were encrusted with jewels.

I also got to witness one of the finest displays of the absurd. I had walked up the mountain and landed on a hill above the backyard of a house, completely dark inside and out. As I sat there looking down into the still back yard with its' dark swimming pool a light came on in the house, then what I still believe to this day was marching band music came on and the French doors opened and I saw a family consisting of what I guess was a mother, father, little girl and a smaller boy came out in rain coats and hats, and they appeared to march around the pool.

They then went back inside, the music ended and the light went out again. It was a lovely show!

Walking down the hill, (now I think this was the same night) a car came up from behind and it was a friend of mine, Arthur Lee, from the group Love. They had been playing around town, most regularly at Bido Lido's on Ivar and another club, The Brave New World I think that one was one Selma. Arthur offered me a ride, and I got into the back seat and I saw an L.P. there that was a picture made of colored drops forming a face. I mentioned this to Arthur a couple of years ago, he decided it must have been his John Coltrane album.

I shall have to settle for that now because since I started this, a couple of years ago, poor Arthur ran into some trouble with the law and ended up in prison for a few years, then the tragic illness that overtook him, leukemia, took his life in July of 2006.

Arthur Lee & I at the Fillmore, San Francisco, 2003

Once back in the house on Ridpath, I think I listened to the *Revolver* album some more and toward the end of the trip I remember some old friends, from school, Linda Levine, Bobby Stroger and his friend Kenny came over. They went into the kitchen and made pizza's on English muffins.

19

Sometimes people who really have no interest to others, unless they too know them, may appear in this narrative. Such is the case with Linda, Bobby & Kenny, but as they were there and I believe anyone, whether famous or not, has some influence on whomever they come into contact with or whatever situation they happen upon, so I feel it right to include one and all.

It was truly a perfect trip. Then reality seeped back, and it seemed so very harsh.

I had gone upstairs, still quite high, I suppose, and the radio was on in one of the rooms. On it was being broadcast the events of the night, the news, or news bulletin. Going on just down the hill there was a riot on the Sunset Strip. This had begun at Pandora's Box, a club on a cement island in the middle of Sunset at Crescent Heights, long gone now.

This riot was later the subject of the film *Riot on the Sunset Strip* and of course the song by Stephen Stills *For What It's Worth*. It was November 1966.

The times they were a'changin.

I remember thinking at the time, "how could such an awful, violent thing be happening in such a beautiful world full of peace, love and pretty colours?"

But it was just the drug.

Or was it?

So, that was one of my forays into the world of psychedelics, but a particularly poignant one. I guess because it was new. I can't really recall Russell's part in it, but that was probably because he was cool enough to see I was doing really well on my own. Also, he had his own trip going.

JohnYork who was curious enough to try Acid but wouldn't quite do it yet, was waiting to see how I came out before he would try it too.

Now that I think of it, I guess I was the guinea pig. But I had already been that for UCLA hadn't I?

It turns out, I was the instigator for many people trying different things over the years, or rather, the water-mark for it. After all, if I could take it and be O.K. why wouldn't other people?

John York and I, 1965

I probably shouldn't be proud of it, and proud isn't the word. It just was the way things went, that's all.

Though it wasn't at all like being a pusher nothing like that. Remember, this was the time of experimenting for all of us, some of us were just more adventurous than others, or more foolhardy. It wasn't drugs then, although technically, it was. It's very hard to put into words, or try to explain to someone who wasn't there.

In this day and age of "just say no" and all the crime and profiteering surrounding drugs, for young people to say, "Hey, it's free, it's love" sounds so far-fetched, and unbelievably naive. But then it was new and the world was nicer, I'm sure. I certainly would not advocate anyone in their right mind to try any of these things now. Pot, without any additives like Angel Dust, is as far as I would go in this frankly very scary world.

Then it wasn't getting high for escapism, it was consciousness expansion and understanding. This sounds today like the biggest cop-out in the world, real hippy-dippy. But really, we were that idealistic and believing.

Unbelievable now. How it all ended up.

All you have to do is listen to the psychedelic music of the day. All lovely and happy and free and peaceful, and all those other hippie hyperboles. Even Barry Maguire's *"Eve of Destruction"* was comparatively upbeat, considering the subject matter. But it wasn't the terror, desperation, despair and violence of a lot of the music today. Of course the drugs are different and the whole mood of the world is not at all conducive to the peaceful times we had to experiment and experience.

I don't wish to be unfair to Generation X, but sorry, we had the best of times. We had the worst of times as well, but not as bad as it is today out there in the real world. It must be horrible to be a teen today.

Of course if they don't know what they missed, how can they miss it?

Some kids have picked up on our music and clothing styles of the 60s and 70s, but they'll never attain the consciousness and ambiance of the times. More's the pity.

I fear that I am beginning to sound like all previous generations do when talking about the younger generation. I know it isn't the same, though, as I really do believe there has not been a generation before or since equal to ours.

I recently made a foray to the places this all took place. The sixties I mean. Gordon and I drove the California coast from San Diego to San Francisco. I'll include this, perhaps, in another chapter, I don't know how it'll all fit together, I started it in 1995 and it's now 1997, July. Anyway we drove to all these places I drove in 1967. It's the 30 year anniversary of the Summer of Love. We stayed in Big Sur, I saw my old cabin in Lime Creek Rd., I saw Nepenthe, Ventana, Monterey, the Highlands Inn in Carmel, all of it. The point I was going to make here however was how the kids are today, in Haight-Ashbury, where I just was again.

I fully expected it to look like all the other streets where kids congregate today, gang attire, crack, the harder edge. Pleasantly, to my surprise they haven't really changed, in appearance anyway, the same tie-dyed, Indian type of apparel, and by the looks on their faces, pot, psychedelics, perhaps Ecstasy, it was more down-played, but they're keeping the look, if not the dream, alive.

A pleasant surprise, the feeling was still there in the streets, only I had gotten older, physically anyway. The only parking space I could find was a Handicapped spot, and I had the placard.

Gordon and I in Haight Ashbury, 1997

Idealistic? Yes. Hopeful? Yes. Innovative? By all means.

We've messed up a lot but we've also made great inroads.

Of course we'll mess up, we're still the experimenters. No wonder a motto of recent years has been "Shit Happens!"

But, the times were ours, perhaps they still are. It was a magical time, we were stardust, we were golden. To borrow from another poet of the times, "When the moon is in the Seventh House and Jupiter aligns with Mars..."

Yes, the Sixties were a good time to grow. Not perfect. There were many casualties, there still are casualties of the ideals we once tried to embrace. The consciousness expansion turned to a dulling. Perhaps it was that reality could never quite live up to the ideal, and for some of the more sensitive of us it was just too painful to see what was happening, so rather than trying to change it anymore against the adversity we all encountered, a lot of us just tried to dull the reality of it a little too much. Trying to keep a blurry remembrance alive in the mind while dulling the hurt makes cynics of us all. So, there was a time of getting high for the sake of getting high, or rather, getting stoned. Many became alcoholics too.

In fact, now that I think of it, the language even changed.

By that I mean the terminology. Where once it was *getting high* it became *getting stoned, out-of-it, fucked-up*.

That's like going from getting on top of it, to letting it get on top of you.

Like losing the control over your own mind and body, relinquishing it to the power of a too strong influence.

No wonder all these twelve-step programs evolved, sort of a race-memory of a communal help-group of a better time.

Instead of going out and embracing the beauty of the world, we became isolationists. Selfishly protecting what was ours.

The era of free-basing attests to this. Of course the world had a lot to do with this as well, and the users excesses.

How can you go out and embrace the beauty in the world when the beauty gets harder and harder to find. When the beautiful things become private property, No Trespassing, or only 'For Sale' or rent?

Then it just got downright ugly and dangerous out there.

I can attest to this on a personal level. Sometime in the early Eighties, after returning from Texas and my sojourn with the rodeo, I hooked up with another old friend, Keith Allison of Paul Revere and the Raiders.

I had known Keith in a roundabout way as the band Paul Revere and the Raiders was the house band for *Where the Action Is,* we may have known each other back then. Keith took over on bass for Phil 'Fang' Volk, but I don't think this was until 1967 or so, and by then I had moved on.

Keith and I are still great friends, he lives now, as then with a woman, Tina who is a producer/director, mainly of commercials. Now that we are all straight and healthy and free of any shackles that cocaine has to offer I feel it alright to mention that free-basing was a big part of our early relationship. It was an experience, we are all fortunate that we got through it. Others weren't so lucky as Richard Pryor could attest to.

Anyway, I hung out with Keith and Tina at their place off the Strip, and later, the scene took it's toll on them and all our finances, as those scenes always do, and they moved to and from various hotel/motel locations until they moved to New York in about 1983.

For a time, Keith moved in with me, ostensibly to clean up some, but the pull got to be too strong again, so he went back to Tina. Now we are all great friends.

I don't want to go into all the experiences this time offered, I don't want to glorify it nor do I wish to vilify it. It was rich in experiences, which today are sometimes funny, sometimes sad to me. But it exemplifies the point I was making about how the times changed too much to be conducive to taking drugs any more, even recreationally. The drugs also no longer lent themselves to being called purely recreational.

Keith Allison

One thing I do feel is worth stating, and that is that no good seemed to ever come from the scene surrounding cocaine. The people and situations tended to be very dangerous.

No matter how things started out there always seemed to be an undercurrent of evil and distrust.

I, for one, lost a car. Someone took off in it while I was sleeping and had a head on collision on PCH. Then the rent-a-car they got to replace it was borrowed by someone else who was going to score. When they returned I learned that they had purchased the coke with the car!

On the 13th of June 1983, I had dropped off my aunt, who was going to visit friends in Ohio, at LAX that afternoon, and had stopped into a pub, the Cat & Fiddle, when it was in Laurel Canyon, not it's present location on Sunset Blvd. where a much nicer clientel prevails. A guy came in with his hand bleeding. I had just gotten back from Houston, and I offered to take him to a hospital. After we got into the car he pulled a knife and made me drive to my house where he terrorized me, he tried to strangle me, and he raped me. I remember thinking that I had to get out of this ordeal alive, so complied, although it disgusted me. I even had to drive him back into Hollywood to keep him from taking my car. It was horrific! He was horrific! I don't really want to go into all the unpleasant details of this ordeal.

The upshot was that I finally reported it to the police, despite being told I'd be killed if I did. Keith (Allison)had phoned from New York and I just burst out crying and I told him the whole story. He insisted that I go to the police. I decided to go but I was humiliated by the police, the hospital, and the District Attorney here in Glendale, who I believe at the time was Marcia Clark, of the O.J. Simpson trial fame. I was literally told that if I prosecuted, I'd be made the guilty one.

Barrel racing

Rodeo days

So, I went back to Texas for a while.

I suppose I should backtrack a bit and explain how Texas came about in my life anyway, not it's origin in a general sense.

My aunt Adeline had married a Texan called Calvin Parker in the 60s.

Cal died in 1980 and when I came out to L.A. again I moved in with Adeline.

I had thus acquired cousins by marriage in Texas who had invited me to come and stay.

These were Betty, Tex and their son Gary Trussel. I had stayed there when I first went but when I returned I meandered into the cowboy life and stayed elsewhere. The rodeo seemed a logical place for the Cavalryman's daughter who was a proficient equestrian and the Richmond/Rosenberg rodeo in Rosenberg, Texas took me on for a spell. I managed to get a buckle for barrel-racing, hence my slight referral to the rodeo and going to and from Texas.

Taking the bull by the horns!

When I returned about a month later I actually saw this son-of-a-bitch who had raped me around town. He seemed to stalk the places I went. I even called the police on him a couple of times, I didn't know who he was but the cops did because I learned later that he was wanted in connection with the Laurel Canyon murders that the porn star John Holmes had taken the rap for. This guy who had brutally raped me worked for the club owner Eddie Nash. This guy is now serving a long sentence for a lot of offences, racketeering and the like.

When I had picked my rapist out of a mug-shot book at the D.A.'s office he had been wanted for a couple of other rapes, but had terrified the other victims into not prosecuting, and the state wouldn't prosecute without the victims testimonies back then. That all changed with O.J. Simpson.

This rapist turned up on my doorstep one hot August night. I went straight in to call 911. I had a gun trained on the door and after he had cut through the screen door and entered the room I was in, I fired. When the police finally arrived, after ten minutes or more and searched the street, no one was around (of course after I fired at him, and the cops took 10 minutes or so to get here, he wasn't hanging around.)

They arrested *me* for firing a gun in city limits. I was cuffed and taken to Olive View for mental evaluation, and treated like a criminal for trying to protect myself.

In the morning I learned that this guy had be arrested and released, thinking that I had blown the whistle on him, he showed up again to teach me a lesson, so I didn't have to spend the whole 72 hours "being evaluated." The only sad but still comic outcome of this episode was that when I finally had gotten all the proper doctors letters, indicating that I was mentally and emotionally competent to own a pistol, this detective told me as he handed me back my property "Here's your gun, but don't use it" I said; "What do I do if I wake up with this guys hand on my throat?" he said in all seriousness "Call us first."!

Luckily he never showed his face in my world again, and whoever you are, AKA Bill Lee, I came through it all right. Better than your life, I should think, and the way you were going you are probably, hopefully, dead by now.

Gary Trussell & I in Texas, 1983

Soon after that incident in 1983 my horse was born (foaled) and waited for me to get around to meeting him. I bought my horse Sun's Dark Chance in 1985 and my life changed 100 per cent for the better.

My horse, Sun's Dark Chance & I

I would ride every night back then, going out for hours and then go to a local Country and Western club called The Forge, two-step, line

30

dance, drink beer and do shots of tequila, just to go home and do it all over again the next day. It worked fine.. With that sort of crowd however, cowboys and bikers, there has to be some tension. I got a tooth knocked out and a truck stolen, all over a guy I liked, J.P and his wife Annette are now great friends. It wasn't show-business, but it was certainly entertaining and earthy for a while.

Now back to when the world was a better place. The sixties of course.

Chapter 4

I used to think nothing of hitchhiking all over California, and beyond. We'd sometimes just take off at a week-end, or anytime in the Summer, before I could drive, and hitch up to San Francisco, sleep in the church hall in Haight-Ashbury, eating the free nut bread and tea they gave us. Never had a problem at all. Diane Horton, Heidi and I were constantly hitching everywhere. Of course, poor, dear Diane went kind of crazy years later, when the rest of us had stopped hitchhiking and would get herself slapped around while hitching through the Canyon, she'd have a black eye or a split lip. No one ever actually figured out what she did to irritate her rides. She was sent to the State of California mental hospital at Camarillo, and when she finally came out and was at a half-way house years later, she killed herself. Whether intentionally or an accidental over-dose we'll never know. She had had a very cold home life. Perhaps now she has found some peace. And love.

I'm getting way off track here, or off onto another track, but that's what memoirs are all about. Going off on tangents, Going off on rants.

It's very cathartic.

So, we had our casualties. Shit happens. It's all part of the experience, and we supposedly learn from ours, and other's mistakes. I still think we had the best times regardless of our detours. If we survived them, all the better. What doesn't kill us makes us, if not stronger at least wiser in the long run.

Cynics, yes. but with a sense of humour, I hope.

I've noticed a lot of people are afraid of their pasts, or guilty about them. I don't understand this. Perhaps it's a form of egotism. Thinking that what you did was any different from what a lot of other people did is really conceited.

This, I've noticed, happens a lot in peoples' relationships, and marriages as well. Friends of mine are actually afraid that their spouses, who weren't part of their past, might actually find out that they had other affairs before them. How silly to think that you can fool your recent husband into thinking you were a virgin who never dated before you met him--at 30 or 40!

If you can't be proud, or at least accept things in your past, then you probably shouldn't have done them in the first place. If you did something you aren't particularly proud of, well, live with it, it was a learning experience. Don't use it as an excuse for being an alcoholic or drug user, or for any other type of sociopathic behaviour. The other thing about all this denial is that it just reinforces the isolationism that took place with the fall of the ideal. If you have nothing else, you have in common the experiences of your youth, of our youth. The most diverse personalities can find a common ground reminiscing about the good old-bad old days.

A lot of ice is broken that way. Very few people will actually look down on you for your past experiences or even your past indiscretions.

Sure, there are always going to be some things we have done that we really wish we hadn't done, something a bit too embarrassing, that's difficult to explain, because when it happened, well, you had to be there to understand...that sort of thing. Those things you might have to gauge your audience before telling your stories, but it doesn't matter in the end, not really.

Someone would have to be incredibly narrow-minded and stupid to judge you today by stereotyping you into a category that your past deeds might denote. "I didn't inhale", should not have been a political issue for Bill Clinton, even if he did inhale.

Quite the contrary. I should think that if you had evolved into some tremendously successful individual from a particularly sordid past that it would be in your favour to divulge what environs you used to inhabit.

It also gives hope to others who are too ashamed of themselves to ever think they will ever amount to anything, so they don't even try.

We are all role models to someone, as I found out not too long ago.

But, more of that later.

Remember the urge you once had to be free of the shackles of normality? What happened? You became the normality.

I'm not advocating the old *"Turn On, Tune in, Drop Out."* Not if you want to function anyway. But don't become the anal-retentive uptight clone of everything we abhorred in our youth either.

The whole idea was to change things in the mainstream. To make a better world for us and future generations. What happened?

Just look around. The greed of the former generations tainted our gene pool somehow and we all conformed a little too much. We are afraid to actually live the dream. Probably because while we were dreaming some other greedy son-of-a-bitch would take away all our opportunities and capitalize on them.

I like the creature comforts that money can buy as much as the next person, and I get as much as I can. But I find that I'm almost embarrassed, or, perhaps, a bit afraid of accumulating too much wealth. It could just change things too much. I don't know. I do know that I have a pretty good life, and though I could certainly do with a better income, I am still doing well for making far below the poverty line.

I recently quit a job.

Yes, I actually went and got a day job, strictly for the money and did very well. It was a thankless sort of telemarketing thing, setting appointments with senior citizens to see something that could help them help themselves. I don't wish to give this company a plug, suffice it to say I did extremely well the first year or so, making over $24,000 just on commissions, then some personal things came up and I had to take a leave of absence for a month and when I returned it was to a different department and the momentum never quite picked up. The sales went down and with it the money and enthusiasm. No motivation really had me feeling trapped and the whole thing went from being a kind of noble cause to being a money-grubbing dirty little business. Then my back started giving me a lot of pain from sitting there all day, well, one day I simply unplugged my headset and walked out. If I hadn't I would have blown a fuse. The stress was too much. So, now I have no income but neither do I have the aggravation and I am happier and I am sure healthier. Something else should present itself and I can be proud of how well I did while the going was good.

Now back to the 60's,(I wish), in my story.

The Broadway/Caroline Charles fashion show tour....

One of the guys in The Bees was called George Caldwell. He had a wife called Mimi who danced with the Gazzarri Dancers, at the club on the Strip. In visiting them with John York I got invited to rehearse with them now and again. From all that dancing and the contacts I made on the Strip, I got a job briefly dancing in the cage at the Whiskey A-Go-Go. Elmer Valentine hired me and I danced during the sets of the house band, which was Johnny Rivers at that time in '65. Unfortunately it didn't last very long, as Mario, the other owner of the Whiskey came back from Chicago or somewhere and he knew me from hanging around, he also knew I was only 15. I see Mario from time to time, whenever I go into the Rainbow Bar & Grill or the Roxy, and it's so sweet. He still makes mention of those times and still apologizes for having to let me go. Says the ABC would have closed him down, not to mention the child labor people.

Mario Maglieri & I at the Whiskey A GoGo's 35th Anniversary party

Relax Mario, it's O.K. It's been over 30 years. I'm over it!

In 1966 Dick Clark started a television show called "*Where the Action Is.*" They would go to all the hip, trendy and in places around Southern California with a current Top 40 act or two. The house band, Paul Revere & The Raiders, would play some of their songs and a lot of other Top 40 tunes and the Gazzarri Dancers would do a little routine, all very hip. As I had been to rehearsals I came along as an alternate dancer when one of the regulars couldn't make it, and the rest of the time I just hung out.

35

I sort of fancied Mark Lindsay of the Raiders. But it was just a "Hi, how are you?" sort of thing that teen-agers get into. I think it got blown apart when he got told my real age. Funnily enough, the same girl who had told on Heidi and I for smoking and starting that fire in the Milliken bathroom told Mark my age, and also a few years later told on Heidi and I for passing out the then legal THC in the Whiskey during a Barry Goldberg Reunion show, but that's another story.

Gordon & I at the Whiskeys' party, 1999

Me as a Go Go dancer, Teen Magazine, 1965

It was at one of the *'Where the Action Is'* tapings, out at the old Yacht Club in Santa Monica on PCH that I met my future. Albeit distant future.

It was April 1966, I think I was dancing that day.

As far as I can recall he started chatting me up. It was all very flattering. A very good looking, polite British singing star. After the show we all piled into my 1955 red and black Plymouth coupe and headed east on Sunset Boulevard. It was already after dark and I remember having to stop along the way to phone home and say I was O.K., and could I stay out a while longer (I may have had a lot of freedom, but I also had a bit of a curfew.) Also I retained my freedom by being considerate and not letting my parents worry where I was. That I was O.K. and that sort of thing worked wonders.

So, I tried to get permission, even had one of his friends get on the phone with my dad, Roger Willis it was, but to know avail, so I dropped them off at the hotel, the Hollywood Sunset, on Sunset and Sweetzer, it later became a retirement hotel The Golden Crest but it's an hotel again now, The Standard.

I cut school either the next day or the day after that, and went by the hotel to see him . I don't recall if it was then exactly, but the way it all went down was we went off to his room to watch TV and smoke a joint. One thing led to another, and lo and behold I lost my virginity. What was really funny at the time was that he and his partner Peter were scheduled to appear on the *Lloyd Thaxton* Show that afternoon. This was a television show where different schools were invited to come and dance to records, They had one guest band, sort of a West Coast *American Bandstand..* So, we got to the television station, I think it was KCOP, which was channel 13 at the time. When we got there I noticed the audience consisted of my class at school, if I had still been going to that school. It was the girls that went to Van Nuys High instead of Grant, but we had been in Milliken Jr. High School.

All of my friends and acquaintances were there and I stroll in with the band. I was high and having just been laid for the first time. It was hilarious, and I took a couple of my friends, Cathy Rowland being one I remember being there, aside, and tell them what I had just been up to. It was a trip.

So, can you guess who it was? Here's a musical hint.

I could *"Go to Pieces"* as a young *"Woman"* in a *"World Without Love."*

Right, Peter & Gordon.

I've always kept in touch through Christmas cards and what not. As of this first writing, I hadn't actually seen Gordon for about 23 years. Now two years after I started writing my memoirs, he's right in the next room. Read on!

Gordon Waller, Peter Asher & I, 1966

Another great circle that has occurred over the years is that a couple of years ago Gordon was involved in writing songs for a soundtrack for a yet-to-be-released, independent film *"James Dean-Race With Destiny."*

He had contacted a few old friends, one of whom was Keith Allison from Paul Revere and the Raiders. They had known each other when Paul Revere & the Raiders played on the same tour with Peter & Gordon in 1964.

So, Keith and Gordon are sitting in my living room, and now John York has become involved playing music with Gordon as well.

So, here's the circle, or connection, or what have you.

I danced on the fashion tour when John York was with the Bees, then danced at the Whiskey A Go Go where Johnny Rivers was the house band, then danced on *"Where the Action Is"* where Keith Allison performs with Paul Revere and The Raiders. Then I meet Gordon. In the 80s Keith and I were thrown together, as it were, for a while. And 30 years later, John York plays with Gordon. Gordon and I are together, Keith is playing with Johnny Rivers and writing a song with Gordon in my living room.

Synchronicity.

On to 1967. The Summer of Love. As I write this now we are coming up to the 30th Anniversary of that magical summer in just one weeks time.

The year 1967 was also the Summer I was supposed to graduate from high school, legally and officially.

Once again, I left before I left.

By this, I mean that the Monterey Pop Festival was happening June 16th, 17th, and 18th and graduation was on the 16th. So I skipped graduation and went to Monterey. They took 4 credits from me and wouldn't give me a diploma in the end, but I had been absent 49 days in my last semester, so I couldn't balk. I left as poet laureate of my senior class. In all these years since then I have never been asked about graduation nor the diploma I was refused. But a hell of a lot of people have asked me about the Monterey Pop Festival.

Of course, it wasn't as simple as just not going to graduation. Or rather, it wasn't graduation that was the issue at all. It was getting my parents to go along with my taking off with a total stranger for three or four days.

I can't recall how I met Michael Vosse nor how he came to offer to take me to Monterey. I just have a vague recollection of going somewhere with some friends, someone called Bruce Campbell comes to mind, as a name only, and I met Michael. He was going to the Festival and that's all she wrote. To this day I cannot say I knew, nor now know, more than that about either Bruce nor Michael. What Michael did? Who knows.

It was really just something I had to do. Like Vegas in '64. So I went. I do remember having to throw scrambled eggs at my father, on the morning of departure. I was a little high strung, I think methadrine was the drug of choice that summer.

Teenagers by definition are a terrible breed for the most part. Well, not so terrible as headstrong, and if not afraid of their parental units, as I wasn't, a bit *out there*.

It was the morning of my intended departure to Monterey, at breakfast, that my dad was going on and on about how I shouldn't, or couldn't go with a virtual stranger to this rock and roll festival for three days. It turned out a lot longer but I was having none of it. I finally picked up a handful of my scrambled eggs and threw them at dear old dad. I left soon after that.

Off we went in Michaels' 1965 yellow Ford Mustang convertible.

Selected memories of the trip were leaving the freeway at Morro Bay to take the coast route, something I still do when traveling north today. Eating at a Mexican restaurant that was in the proprietors home, something that isn't seen, or perhaps allowed today. It was a restaurant in on the lanai of this family's home. Very clean and nice and incredible home cooked Mexican food.

I remember Michael opening the connecting door of the motel room (The Flamingo in Monterey), and saying to its' occupants: "Behold the youth of America!" Or something to that effect. You see, I was busy trying to get off on some Ritalin at the time. Don't get me wrong. I wasn't some sorry-assed junkie, nodding and scratching through the seedy under-pinnings of society with tracks up and down the road map of veins. No, I was just a young hippie, happy and free and experimenting with the things this brave new world had to offer. We had no guidelines or negative role models as yet. Heaven forbid that I would give up my newfound freedom to become a slave to pushers and the habitual hell they peddled. Nothing was going to govern my actions and sentence me to a life of hum-drum regularity. Not even a regularity of <u>having</u> to do a recreational drug.

I just wanted to get that straight as there will be numerous references to drugs throughout this story. Fortunately for me they were, for the most part fun and harmless. Unfortunately, for others, they were not. But this is my story. Also, as I've said, this was a time when the whole scene, drugs not withstanding, was 180 degrees from what it became in the years that followed. And nothing at all like the horror story it has become today.

If speed was the drug of choice that summer, LSD was the drug of choice that decade.

Chapter 5

Augustus Stanley Owsley III, a brilliant, if unorthodox chemist, dropped it from the sky to the place beneath, and the Monterey fairgrounds soon had ground-in purple mixed with the very earth. Monterey Purple. But it wasn't all getting high. There was the music and the love and the people. From the moment the Association hit he stage with *"Along Came Mary"* the Festival was officially underway. The talents of Jimi Hendrix, Janis Joplin, the Who, and all the previously unheard San Francisco bands, the Jefferson Airplane, Big Brother and the Holding Company (with Janis Joplin), all these San Francisco acts were only previously heard if you had been to the Fillmore West or the Avalon Ballroom. It sounds hippy-dippy and corny to try to speak of it all today. But it really was a whole feeling that pervaded that magical summer. It was then that the album *"Sgt. Pepper's Lonely Hearts Club Band"* was released. In fact, it was played for the first time that weekend over the radio. We were driving through Big Sur when that happened. Yes, on Acid!

We went to a restaurant called Nepenthe, a place called the Esalon Center, with the sulfur baths overlooking the Pacific Ocean with the glowing red plankton in the moonlight. It was magical. I saw a six-toed cat at Nepenthe. Sometime later, back in L.A., Michael Vosse showed up at my door in Benedict Canyon with a little black and white kitten. She had six toes and I called her Nepenthe of course. I don't know where he got her, or if she was the same kitten from Big Sur. People did stuff like that then. It was cool.

The other new release that weekend was Procol Harum's *"Whiter Shade of Pale"*. It went well with the fog in Big Sur, very well.

Then there was the night the Rolling Stones' Brian Jones had a party at the Highlands Inn, in Carmel. He wasn't performing at the festival. He was just hanging out with Niko of the Velvet Underground, Andy Warhol's group out of New York. It was late and I couldn't get back to Monterey, so I went to the desk and the night clerk said he'd give me a room, there was another girl who needed to crash, so we shared a room, but we had to be out before the morning shift came on. No charge. In the morning, we went around to the pool side and there was a champagne brunch going on for the guests of the hotel. Thanks to the night clerk and the room key I still had we had a great breakfast. A few of the other of the late night stragglers of the previous nights revels wandered in and followed suit. When it came time to pay the check I signed my middle names, Eve Lindsay, along with the room key it was fine. Hey, it worked. I think all of us then hitch-hiked back to Monterey.

Then came Sunday.

Ravi Shankar was greeting the dawn on stage, and the previous few days caught up with me, for not only was I partying and having fun, I was working as well. More of this later.

I went back to the motel to lie down and found the room filled to capacity with people I both knew and didn't know. That was sometimes a drawback during this time, we were all so damn communal we sometimes got over-run with new friends who took up all the room, food, dope, clothes, telephones, records, etc. You get the picture.

I guess everyone was a bit tired and the prospect of having an actual room opposed to sleeping in the fairgrounds was appealing. Plus it was raining.

I managed to find space on the floor of the long closet. There were no clothes in it, maybe a knap-sack or two, and I slept with the mellow sounds of Sitar, Tabla and rain wafting through the window from across the street at the Festival.

People may talk of Woodstock and all the other festivals, but this was the festival, not to end all festivals but to begin all festivals. We were the core group, as it were. We were the ones who had started all this at the Be-Ins and Love Ins in Fern Dell here in L.A. in Griffith Park. The little mini festivals. An early attempt at tribal togetherness and celebration of being young and new and having something to say. We passed the word to the rest of the country and the world at Monterey and from this one summer of love, peace and music came Woodstock and all the other festivals. Personally I didn't think Monterey ever had an equal in innocence and originality. Look what happened by the time Altamont came along in 1969, with kids getting crushed and stabbed by security. The Stones' must regret, in hindsight, hiring the Hell's Angels as security!

The Isle of Wight Festivals in the early '70's, a few years down the road, were pleasant enough, but never quite attained that first very personal experience, for everyone.

The entire year of 1967 had that quality. It was a feeling of a new beginning while at the same time being a once in a lifetime shot at getting it right. Life, that is.

My friend Michael Mitchell, 'Scottish Michael' he was when I first knew him in 1965, a friend of Heidi's. He summed up that feeling when he said recently that 1967 was the year we all went everywhere and did everything and never had a penny in our pockets. Yet we had everything we wanted. Weird and wonderful.

But, back to the reality, such as it was, of the festival itself and how it impacted my life.

It so happened that Derek Taylor, from the Beatles days, whom I had met in Las Vegas in '64, was doing Public Relations there and I got myself hired on. Helping out with this and that. It was through this that I met various people in the business, as someone also in the business, not a fan as such, or as they came to be called groupies. No, never a groupie.

Funnily enough I just thought, even though the Sixties were the time of free love, "make love not war" and all that, and this was the summer of love, I wasn't personally involved in nor did I really see anything sexual going on whatsoever, not at the festival anyway. So much for publicity, I am sure it was going on but not overtly so. Perhaps more with the 'older' crowd. You know, 20!

We recently lost Derek Taylor to cancer at the end of 1997. He was a great man, and will be missed. He also, will be well remembered.

Another thought. Though I don't recall any overt sexual behavior going on, I know it was all through this time. It sure was lucky that no diseases were about that couldn't be cured with penicillin Not like today and AIDS, everyone would be sick or dead if that had been around then.

If I think on it I suppose I was sexually active from the age of 16 onwards. After Gordon came Michael (the Scottish one). Heidi and I shared. It seemed a really innocent time with sex then. No big thing just something to do to be close and loving and not get into any heavy things. We were all just really good friends. Relationships were very open to non-existent!

The festival ended and I kept returning to Big Sur and stayed in a house in Lime Creek Road for a spell. School was out for good. The modeling thing had sort of soured on me when the head of one of the teenage magazines called me in just around my 18th birthday to let me know that the jobs were getting harder to get, but if I'd like to come to his place one night we could 'discuss' it. Yeah, discuss it indeed. Discuss THIS buddy! No sexual harassment laws in those days.

I guess I was sort of bored with things. It was not just me though there was a mood that came upon L.A., I can't put my finger on it, a restlessness.

There was more somewhere and once again I had to find a way to get to it.

Things did, indeed, begin to change. And by 1969, I had decided I just had to go back to England. I had, after all, been born there. Once again my parents managed to come through. Not really affluent themselves, what featured actors' are? They came up with a passage on P.&O.'s (Pacific and Orient Line) Flagship, the S.S. Canberra. This was facilitated by an old friend of my mothers', the writer of the *"Blondie and Dagwood"* series, Karen De Woolf. Don't ask me how. My parents always tried to grant my desires. Not in a spoiled kind of thing. I know they loved me unconditionally. But sometimes I get the feeling from my mother, even now, that it's almost kind of a fear that if I wasn't happy, I might just cut them off without a backward glance. Not that I ever would have. But I see how they could have thought that. I do have the ability to shut out, exclude, turn my back on or whatever, any situation that is no longer of any use to me.A no crying over spilt milk thing. This is always on an impersonal level, hardly ever to anyone within my close personal circle. So I don't see how they may have felt so insecure about me, as this is only my way of carrying on doing what I need to get done without any outside interference. Thinking on this again now, a few years later, I think I was just being considered a growing girl with ideas on how I wanted to lead my life. Being the rather understanding parents they were, and still are, mum at least, they also had a good grasp of how difficult their parents made it for them to continue on with their growth process unimpeded. They didn't want to do the same thing to me with all the remorse and guilt that can put on a kid.

Setting sail. Two friends, Adeline, me, dad and mum. 1969.

So, on the 13th July 1969 I set sail with all my worldly possessions from the L.A. Harbor in San Pedro with my family and a few well chosen friends at my side. The Bon Voyage party was: Cathy and Georgia Rowland, Heidi Friars, Michael Mitchell, and as I was reminded only a couple of years ago, Mark Kline was also there, but he took the pictures and wasn't actually in any of them so I didn't recall. Mark is still a friend and was at Gordon's 60th birthday party with his daughter Callie this past June (2005). He was a friend of Michael Mitchells' at the start and still is. Mark has always been there it seems. I even used to work on shows with him during my 'movie' years. He was a grip on "N.Y.P.D. Blue" amongst other productions. Recently, these past couple of years (we are already in 2007), we have been in each others company again. He and his daughter Cally have been around when Michael comes down from San Francisco to see the Who. Most recently in November of 06, at the Hollywood Bowl and February of 07 at the Long Beach Arena.

Heidi Friars, Michael Mitchell & I. S.S. Canberra, July 1969.

My journey was not by any means uneventful. I managed to make my presence felt, though really quite unintentionally. I began hanging around with the crew. Not the officers, much to my mother's dismay, but the officers were so very dull. Extremely polite and correct people always seem very dull and boring to me. No, the crew. Mainly my table steward, Mick Brooks, and his mates. Mick came from Watford and was a Gemini, that's about all I remember. For a time, I used to go down to Southampton when his ship was in and pass the time. All else I remember of him was his showing up at my door in London saying he'd left his wife. I had to send him on his way as it had been, after all, only a shipboard romance, and barely that. We'd all had a good time in the various ports we'd visited. The crew always knows the better, earthier bars and places to go to.

A great one in Panama was reached by mean streets filled with guerrilla soldiers leaning against parked cars with automatic weapons at hand. The bar was a huge room with sawdust on the floor and swinging doors. I remember a woman, a midget, dancing with a man with a peg leg. These were parts of town the ship actually warned passengers not to go to. How boring it must have been for the rest of the passengers!

Back to the ship. Hanging out with the crew, I was often down in their quarters, drinking beer and partying. Ships have water-tight drills, where they close off certain sections and you can't leave till the drill is over with. It was during one of these drills that my cabin steward noticed that my bunk had not been slept in, and being a good Goanese cabin steward he had to report it. This, however, sets off a routine that managed to get me written up in the log book.

It seems that when a passenger can't be located they have to turn the ship around in a figure-eight in the middle of the ocean. This they did, costing the Company some £480! Strike one. The next event with THE COMPANY was after going ashore in Lisbon. Running late I got into a taxi, "Embarko blanco!" I direct the driver in my best Spanish, to no avail.

Of course they speak Portuguese in Lisbon. Anyway I am duly dropped off at the white ship', and while standing on deck watching another white ship going through he harbour to the open sea, one of the other observers at the rail with me says "there goes the Canberra", to which I say something like, "No this is the Canberra, I'm sailing on the Canberra."

The upshot of this tale being that I was dropped off at the wrong ship, and that my ship was at that moment sailing off into Lisbon Harbor! I was on another of P.&O.'s line, the Iberia.

A quick call out to the ship and I was taken out on the Pilot boat.

Strike Two.

The third event could really just be called a misdemeanor. As I got back to the ship in Cherbourg after the gangway had been removed prior to sailing, no biggie. But the look on the third officers' face! I'd been the bane of his existence the entire trip.

The crew called him The Fly.

When we finally did reach the Port of Southampton, rather than remain on board in order to go through Customs in the morning and enter the country legally, I jumped ship with some of the crew. One of Mick's mates had family living in Guildford, so I snuck off with them and went to his parents' place. I was given an old feather bed in the loft of their thatched cottage, and in the morning we cycled over to a pub for a Plowman's lunch and ale. Then I was snuck back on board so I could enter the country legally. Thanks to the family of crew member Guy Broughton, I had a disembarkation to remember, two of them!

Me & some ships crew . Cherbourg

Me, Guy Broughton and some of the crew.

So, here I was in England, land of my birth, 19 years old with letters of introduction in hand.

Herbert Newmark was to be meeting me. Although he was referred to as my godfather, I believe he came by that title as a result of being the second husband, now widower, of my godmother Maggie Bennett, whom I don't recall ever meeting. I guess that's what happens when you're Christened in London and then leave the country for almost 19 years.

Off we went into the English countryside in his vintage Jaguar. Herbie had a watch making business in Switzerland and a pig farm in Sussex. It was to the pig farm we went, in Rudgwick.

This was rather a new experience for the both of us. I am sure he had never been around a young person before, and I certainly had not been in a very proper English country house with a formal garden and a housekeeper. I believe we dressed for dinner, when alone. It was a trip, it was nice too. One thing that strikes me as idiosyncratic was that shortly after my arrival there the newspaper headlines were all of the Tate/LaBianca killings. It was a case of "...you can check out anytime you want, but you can never leave."

I believe I have already touched on the subject of my friend Heidi and the father of her baby being "Bummer" Bob Beausolais of the

Manson family. I hope Heidi doesn't mind my bringing this up, but she made no secret of it ever, and now that she lives in another state and won't communicate with any of her old friends any more, I guess it's still O.K., she'd have to call and tell me if it wasn't and I don't think she wants to be bothered with doing that. Sorry Heidi if it offends, but it's all true, my old friend.

Another connection with the Manson family was that I attended Grant High School with a couple of the Manson girls, I believe Linda Kasabian, Patricia Krenwinkle and Susie Frome were also enrolled there. I didn't hang out with them. Frankly, I found Charlie a little too weird for my tastes and I wasn't a follower of anybody but being in the same environs our paths did cross, and times being what they were it was accepted. I mean in as much that if you saw someone you knew and they asked for a ride and it wasn't out of your way, well, as the old saying goes, "Ass, Gas or Grass--no one rides free!"

So, as things would have it I sometimes gave people a ride and some of these people, in hindsight, well I probably should have let walk. But I didn't, and nothing untoward happened, perhaps I was just lucky. But thinking back of the times I gave rides up to Sharon Tates' house and was asked to come in and get high or something, sometimes asked by Charlie's buck-knife, he felt it punctuated his points and desires to flick open a buck knife he always had at hand. I consider myself fortunate I wasn't there and asked to drop anyone off up there on that fateful night in August of 1969. Or worse, come in!

Then again as I was in no way any part of that evil circle of lunatics (sorry guys, but...) I probably wouldn't have been asked anyway. Thank God.

Back to Sussex.

After a few days of acclimatizing, as it were, I joined Herbie on what I suppose was a business trip. His chauffeur dropped me off at the airport. Herbie met me at the airport in Geneva. I had enough time at Geneva Airport while waiting for Herbie to walk into a bank there and open a Swiss numbered account. I had only heard of numbered Swiss accounts in books and the movies and must have thought it terribly romantic or something so I took £5 and opened an account. All very well and good but I have no idea at all which bank it was nor what the number of the account was. So, somewhere there has been interest accruing since 1969 on my £5!

This grand tour, though only of Switzerland really, was quite a high class affair, now that I look back on it. We went to Cran Sur Sierre, which was a very posh resort. Here we were with his business partner and his wife, the Rothchild's. We drove all over the place. One day in Zermatt, taking the train up to Gornergratt, the climb was so steep I kept passing out due to the thin air at those altitudes. No great discovery, but it was the first time in my experience. Once at the top though we were even with the Matterhorn, but try as I might I just couldn't get a clear picture of the peak without a cloud obscuring part of that famous outline.

I can't recall offhand all the other locations we visited. There was a place on Lac Morat right out of another time, we ate on the terrace and went out on a small boat and swam in the silty-bottomed lake. It was a place of covered bridges and gingerbread houses. Very Hansel and Gretel.

At Mont Blanc, Switzerland

Herbert Newmark at the Matterhorn, 1969.

Chapter 6

After we returned to England, I had a few more duty calls to make as it were, and so bid a fond farewell to Herbie and went to Eastbourne to visit with my fathers' old nanny, though she had actually been housemaid to his mother, Muriel, when he was a little boy. Her name was Winnifred Kenward.

I was escorted through a more fundamental England with Winnifred. Marks & Spencer, Woolworths' that sort of thing. We took a Green Line double-decker bus to Hastings. I saw the Baiuel Tapestry, my Grand-mother Muriels' grave and the clock at Greenwich.(GMT).

I had a room at the top of her house, and the nearest bathroom was three flights down, but there was a chamber pot under the bed. One night I had taken a diuretic and as you can imagine that bed pan filled up rather quickly. Along about dawn, or a little after, I decided I had better empty it, out the window. Onto the postman as it turned out. Poor guy. I heard an exclamation from below, I don't think he knew what hit him, but I guess he came to find out he had a pretty good idea.

On to the next leg of my travels, not because of the postman, but it was time to move on.

I next traveled by train to Scotland to meet my only other blood relatives on earth. The only ones' I know of anyway.

Brigadier William "Billy" Steele, the son of my fathers' fathers' brother, or his first cousin. He had been in the military forever, in the Coldstream Guards. A very well known regiment, historically.

There had always been a photograph on the wall at home of my paternal grandfather, George Frederick Steele, who had been killed way back in about 1915 in Ypes during the First World War. Imagine my surprise when I got off the train in Edinburgh to be met by his spitting image!

The Steele's. Julian, Mary, Brig. William & Anthony.

The family home, Corner House, was a mansion near the Firth of Forth in North Berwick. The main part of it was more like a museum, and I felt there should be velvet ropes to keep people away from the furniture and object d'art, but really they were a very down-to-earth bunch of country folk. Tweedy, 'huntin', fishin' and shootin'. Billy was the president of St. Andrews Golf Club and I managed to dig up a goodly portion of the Firth trying to hit a few golf balls myself. They took me on many day trips.

When I say *they* I mean my cousins. This was Billy, his wife Mary, and their two sons Anthony, who was studying animal husbandry at an Agricultural College in Perthshire, and Julian, who was still in school, at Eton, and when I last heard, he had joined his fathers' regiment, the Coldstream Guards.

We went to Bass Rock, which was covered in birds and bird excrement, with a lighthouse we went to the top of. On the way down though I had to sit to descend the rest of those steep spiraling stairs on my ass, I guess I had a slight case of vertigo.

We went to Perth, where Billy and Mary were re-furbishing a house. There it was I squatted on some stingy nettles while peeing and learned that a Dock leaf would cure it, and that Dock leaves always grow near stingy nettles.

We attended the Edinburgh Tattoo at Edinburgh Castle. It was quite a spectacle. Also many other little diversions. It was very nice. One more house to visit. This time I had a glimpse of London as I was to meet up with Mrs. Tomkinson in the lunch room of Peter Jones Department Store in Sloane Square. I don't know really who these people were in relation to me and my family. They were a largish family and lived just outside London. I stayed there for an undetermined length of time. I don't recall my stay there being particularly enjoyable, or really anything, so I shall move on, as I did in fact.

On to London and to form a life of my own.

What I did was to get a newspaper and sit in front of the Chelsea Potter, a trendy pub in the Kings Road, and found a bed-sitting room in South Kensington. This was no bigger than a ships cabin on the Canberra, with a basin, a wardrobe, a chest of drawers. a small desk-like table and chair, and a twin bed. There was a loo down the hall and the bathroom was two flights up. Being in the basement I didn't have to worry about dumping anything on the postman so that was all right. There was a little closet like a cupboard outside my door and when I opened the two doors together I had a little more space. This closet contained a hot plate, a small oven and an electric kettle, so it served me as a kitchen. The ice box was the window ledge. It cost a mere £2-10s per week and I soon had a job in the Pimlico Road at a furnishings store called Casa Pupo. They sold imported rugs, lamps, etc. from Spain and Portugal. Pupo, yes there was such a person, was a colorful, but dour Spaniard who insisted we all could only wear black, white or grey, so as not to detract from his colourful surroundings.

It was here I met a girl who became my flat-mate for the next few years, her name was Fiya Hunt. Fiya had a flat in Cheyne Place, up the road from Mick Jagger and Marianne Faithful in Cheyne Walk. Fiya shared her place with her Boxer dog Huckleberry and her Lebanese boyfriend Fawzi. The job and the bed-sit in South Kensington both lasted about six weeks. I think the job ended when the delivery van driver named Tony got caught delivering rugs and stuff that hadn't been bought through the proper channels, I don't know for sure, but I think Fiya was also involved in this. I may have, inadvertently , been involved as well. Or I just quit, no matter, once again it was time to move on. I could do better than £10-15-5 per week. Oh, and 15' (shillings) in Luncheon Vouchers, redeemable at sandwich shops and the like.

So I moved in with Fiya and her dog and boyfriend. I was duly installed in the living room, with its sofa/day-bed type of thing. Looking back on my 12 1/2 years in Britain it seems I spent most of my time sleeping in the living rooms of wherever it was I was living. I guess it was due to space, and who had the lease on the flat.

Fiya had been married to a civil engineer (as opposed to an uncivil one...?) and had lived in Malaysia, Borneo, Australia, Singapore and all those Colonial sort of places. She was of the cocktail set of the widespread British Colonists, and she was older than I, though only six years or so. I on the other hand...well we should all know something about me by now shouldn't we?

Over a short time I suppose I introduced Fiya to the magical world of hippies and parties and recreational drugs. She caught on fast and was soon rolling those three-skinned hash joints and dropping acid at the drop of a hat.

Fiya Hunt

LSD was really just starting to seep into Britain. While it had been a staple over here in the States for almost a decade by this time, it was only becoming trendy in London in the very late Sixties.

Without touting it at all, it came to me. I guess as water seeks its own level.

Another girl who had worked with me at Casa Pupo, one day approached me and asked if I'd like to make some spare cash. She knew these rich Egyptians and all I had to do was go meet this guy for drinks and he would pay. Sure, I thought, but being adventurous I went along, with her accompanying me the first time. It turned out to be Michael Al-Fayed. He and his brothers Mohammed and Ali were the exiled nephews of King Farouk. I was 19, what did I know or care of all that?

I didn't really appreciate how nice Michael was trying to be towards me. He wanted company sometimes, that's all. I would go over to their penthouse in Park Lane, the very chi chi expensive part of town, and have dinner and he would give me presents, and when I left he gave me an envelope, which was full of money. It seemed like a good deal to me. I was really horrid to him, quite petulant and rude, and I used to give away the little gifts. What a fool I was as they were the likes of Piaget watches and bottles of Joy perfume. I sent a lot of the gifts to my Mother. I slept with him a couple of times, although it wasn't a condition of anything though. It was very odd, really.

He had a nephew named Dodi, he was Mohammeds' son and he seemed like a little boy to me.

He was 12 or 13 I guess. At dinner parties I was to be his escort, or dinner partner, or whatever.

Once I had bronchitis rather badly, and Michael sent me to his house in Genoa so I could recover where there was better weather. It was just me and the chauffeur and housekeeper, and I had carte blanche at any shops in town. Immature fool that I was, I bought a small cassette player and a pair of boots, got bored and went back to London. He was always calling and asking if I'd like to fly over in his private plane to shop in Switzerland or somewhere, and I'd decline. I wanted to stay in London and party with my friends.

I guess I was not cut out to be a kept woman. He must have really liked me, and I was just downright blind to the fact that he was enamored of me. Sorry Michael, I was just an immature kid looking to get her rent paid sometime.

I hadn't thought of the Al-Fayed's in years. Every now and then my mother would mention that Dodi was producing films and I should get in touch, or that Mohammed owned Harrod's. I just didn't think I wanted to rekindle that instance in my past.

In August (1997) all the names and faces were everywhere when poor Dodi and Princess Diana were killed in a tragic car crash in Paris. Rest in Peace guys.

Fiya and I soon had a conglomeration of friends from around the Chelsea area. All the young, trendy, fashionable people of the day. When most of these found I was a seasoned pro, (in the LSD department) they soon asked if I'd be the guide on their first trips, and why not. This went on for years. It was really quite harmless fun and I've still to have any adverse effects from any of it. The so-called experts always were threatening, or promising, flashbacks, but I have yet to confirm any of their findings.

London was still swinging in the early Seventies. It was Blaises, The Pheasantry, The Speakeasy, and the Ad Lib. For this moment in time it was The Revolution in Bruton Place . We were regulars there. It was also the place where I re-met someone who was to change the course of my life over the next decade and beyond.

It must have been early summer as I was off to Ibiza for the first time. My twin friends Michael and Nigel Butcher had discovered this island paradise on a previous occasion. They told me all about it and how I should accompany them that year. It must have been 1970.

On the night prior to my leaving for Spain, I was at the Rev (as it came to be called), and who should I run into but good old Keith Moon from the Who and that magical time in Monterey. He had been very attentive all evening and when 4 am rolled around and the club was closing he asked where I was going. "Home" I said, "I'm off to Ibiza in the morning ." "Why?" asks Keith, "To get some sun." I reply. "I have the sun at my house." Was his reply, the almost Leo. I didn't pursue my inquiry into what he meant and went off into the pre-dawn to Ormonde Gate, and the boat train from Victoria Station in the morning.

Michael Butcher and I in Ibiza, 1970.

When I returned I realized what he had meant. Having recently become separated from his wife, Kim, he was living just off the Kings Road in Jubilee Place, and had a giant sun painted on the wall. We met up again at one or other of the haunts around London.

We were soon seeing quite a bit of each other. The months since our chance encounter at the Revolution had held a great adventure in Ibiza and a trek through Morocco, with us having to hitch-hike back from Malaga to Alicante as our ride was going up the west coast of Spain to Cadiz. I was traveling with three Americans and a Canadian guy I had met in Wauna's bar in Ibiza. The Americans were departing back to America when we reached Spain again after our trip through Morocco. We got back all right, but I had a slight case of Cholera due to my not having gotten the booster to the vaccination I had on entering Morocco. But, it too passed with no really serious consequences.

Chapter 7

That winter, of 1970 my parents decided I wasn't planning on returning to L.A. anytime soon, so, surprise, surprise, they sold the house in Benedict Canyon and took a ship over. They stayed with Fiya and I in Ormonde Gate for a while. I think Fiya gave them her room and went to stay with her boyfriend, or someone's boyfriend somewhere. Then my dads' old friend and partner from the BBC, Cecil Madden gave them the loan of his place in Chelsea.

Keith by now had moved into a house in Bywater Street just across Kings Road from Ormonde Gate. So, we all know where I was spending most of my time.

He was living there with Chalky, the driver of his lavender Bentley, and Chalky's girlfriend, whose name I can't remember. It was a pleasant little group. Quite domesticated really. It wasn't at all as crazy as I've heard it rumored to be in others' speculations; more like a coed dormitory or something. Nigel, of the twins, decided we were really cool and dropped in unannounced often. One unrelated incident involved Nigel taking a flaming chip-pan off the stove and running to the front door with it only to open the door to a wind that blew the flaming fat all over him. Quite nasty really. First and second degree burns all over his hands, face and upper body. He looked like the invisible man for ages, all swaddled up in bandages.

I mention this only to show how normal life was there really. No big differentiation between pop stars and everyday people. I have always been amazed when people I speak with are so impressed by some of my friends, as though they are gods or some sort of mystical creatures. We were all just a bunch of young kids, some of which had cooler jobs than others, but our down time consisted of the same kind of stuff. Other than having Keith throw a bottle through the occasional TV screen as a comment on the programming, and having to explain it to Radio Rentals, (you would rent televisions in England back then.) other than an incident like that once in a while, we was just folks.

Along about then, I had my 21st birthday.

I had been taking acid a lot that holiday, and for the past 7 years or so, and we had all taken it to go with my parents to midnight Mass on Christmas Eve and then probably again. I know I took it on my birthday, and was high during a party my parents threw for me. All was going well, I guess. Everyone was very loaded and generally having a good time, not laid-back, but talking and dancing, etc. I recall thinking it was kind of stuffy then the next thing I knew I was at St. George's' Hospital with a tracheotomy needle in my throat. It seems the Vagas nerve and the thyroid gets affected by a lot of psychedelics that have speed in them, and I had had a lot of psychedelics. But, no problem, right?

The dates escape me, but my parents found a really nice ultra-modern mews house off Smith Street in Chelsea. Woodfall Street it was called, and still is.

Fiya and I gave up the flat in Ormonde Gate, and I moved my stuff into Woodfall Street, and this time I actually had a room of my own.

Keith had bought a house in Chertsey, Tara House, and got a new driver, Dougall (Peter Butler) Kim's Mum Joan, her son Dermott and Keiths' daughter Mandy were installed into the residence and I had farther to go to be with him.

Life went on.

The Who purchased a quadraphonic recording studio in Thessaly Road in Battersea, and called it Ramport.

One night at the Speakeasy, sitting in the restaurant drinking the inevitable brandy and ginger ales and waiting for some scampi and creamed spinach from Luigi, Keith told Wiggie, (John Wolff) a long time long ago employee of the band, that he should give me a job at Ramport. He was called Wiggie as he had no hair due to Alopecia.

So he did. Give me a job, that is.

There was a slight conflict of interest, as I recall. There was this woman named Penny Gillman, who as it so happens had been the daughter of a man my father had been at school with. I think my fathers first girlfriend, as a 13 year old or something was H.C. Gillmans' sister, Susan.

Penny was a rather large, businesslike sort, very mannish, with an undeveloped sense of humor. She had worked at Track Records, which was Kit Lamberts' and Chris Stamps' label and management company that managed the Who and Jimi Hendrix, among others.

I had actually had dinner at Pennys' flat when I first arrived in London, another duty call as it were. All long before this Ramport thing came about.

I don't know what it was exactly but she did not take kindly to my suddenly taking over a spot I think she reckoned would be hers, namely running the workings of the studio from the front reception area. I wasn't aware of the conflict particularly at the time, but looking back on it there was a definite hostility there towards me, the young upstart. I think she was in some way jealous of my being with Keith and the others. She just couldn't let go of her stiff demeanor enough to let herself have any fun. Sorry Penny.

Funny how an impression of a situation will suddenly come to you a full quarter of a century after the fact.

Once installed in Ramport, I came to work each morning and fielded calls to Wiggie and Cy (Cyrano is David Langston, named for his nose, I believe) and if Kit Lambert or Chris Stamp were there, to them as well. It was just a studio in the making in those early days. There wasn't even a desk (board) installed in the control room as yet and the beginning of the making of the album *Quadrophenia* was done via a video camera set up in the studio while Ronnie Lanes' Mobile studio was parked out at the curb, with Ron Nevison at the desk (or board) depending on which side of the Atlantic you come from or reside in.

Cyrano & I.

When the desk was finally installed we were all in the control room and Pete (Townsend) was out in the studio, when it was all connected up to the twelve 100 watt JBL or Kenwood (they kept changing) speakers, Pete said something like, "O.K. lets see how it sounds", and let loose a chord that immediately had everyone's nose and ears bleeding. No one had checked, and the level was up to 140 decibels. I have a ruptured ear drum to this day.

So much for occupational hazards!

Roger Daltrey & I.

It was more fun than work traditionally is. There is a story to go with each day. Heaven help me if I can put them in any order, but they surface now and again.

Come to think on it, it really is amazing we all lived through it. Or rather that as many of us lived through it as did.

John Entwistle & I.

There were so many detours that my life took. I got involved with a group of people, I don't remember how, where or why. I went to the Isle of Wight Festival, the Hendrix one, with the Who, by helicopter, I may have met up with these people then, or not. Another memory from that time was right after the festival hanging around at Chris and Jeanette Wood's flat in Notting Hill Gate. Chris played flute with the group Traffic, they chipped at heroin and I believe Chris died in 1983 of an overdose.

David Rogers, Chris Wood, Jeanette Jacobs & I.

Anyway, after the festival a bunch of us were over at Chris' place. Hendrix was there with his German girlfriend of the moment. I think Jeanette had once been Jimi's girlfriend as well. And so it was that Jimi had to go, he had an important meeting to re-sign a contract the next day. That was the last time anyone saw him alive, he died the next morning. Got a handful of downers instead of uppers is the way I heard it.

But I digress. I lived for a time in the basement flat of a house in Fulham. This must have been around 1972 or so. The guy whose flat it was dealt coke. They lived in the ground floor and upper two stories of the house. Robbie felt he was attracting too much attention from the law and moved out for a time. I did as well. I had come back one afternoon to get some clothes and heard movement upstairs. Going up to look, there was the little brother of a girl Robbie had been seeing. He was with this woman with scales, drugs and all sorts of paraphernalia. I told him to clean it up and get out and started back down the stairs only to be met with a whole row of uniformed coppers from the Chelsea division! 'ello,'ello, 'ello!

I protested that what they might find had nothing to do with me, to no avail. Off to jail we went. First to Chelsea, then because there were no WPC (Women Police Constables) I went to Hammersmith. Ugh!

After a trial at the Old Bailey I was totally exonerated. I simply told the truth to those be-wigged magistrates. Upon hearing that the half pound of cocaine they found there was 83% pure, I protested that though I have been known to use the drug I had nothing to do with that and was a bit put out hearing it was so pure. The Magistrates admonished me and then said "This young lady of impeccable character obviously has nothing to lose by telling the truth and shaming the devil."

I got lucky!

Before all this however I jumped bail and split for Ibiza, where I kept getting telegrams, which I still have, from both Mooney and one from Gordon, pleading with me to return and face the music. The whole reason I had moved into Fawcett Street was because of an argument with Keith, so he admonished me to return as "life in London is lagging without you...." Gordon simply told me to come home at once and call him. I don't recall which I did. But home I came and faced the music, and won.

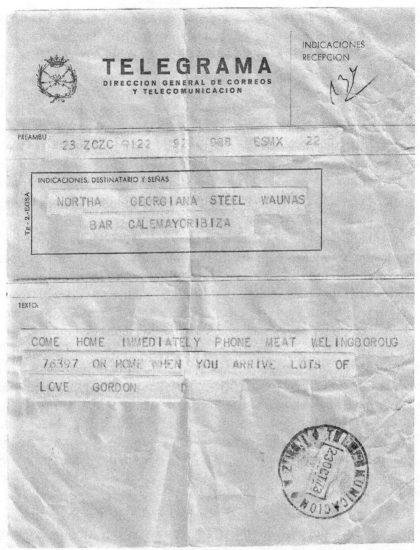

Telegram from Gordon.

So, back to the relatively safe haven of the music business and Ramport.

I recently found out that I was instrumental in bringing a couple of people together from that time, also that I had actually been a role model for a bunch of the local girls who lived in the Council Flats adjacent to Ramport.

It was the strangest thing.

In a whole other time and place I was around all these people again, after almost 20 years.

I had gone off to Las Vegas to see Roger Daltrey perform the Whos' music with a 60-piece orchestra at the Aladdin Hotel. All this is already in story form, so I shall just out-line it here.

It was John Entwistle's 50th birthday on October 9th of 1994, and through circumstances beyond my control [sure] I went to Vegas to see the show and spend his 50th birthday with John and all my old friends.

A few days later, in L.A., after seeing a film with the girl who had suggested we go to Vegas in the first place, (as it turned out one of those friendly opportunists who buddy's up to you for an ulterior motive, she also was house sitting and my telegram from Keith to me in Ibiza hasn't been seen since) this reason being I am friends with people she wanted to get next to. So, this night after the film, she suggests going for a drink at Ma Maison, I should have suspected this, but...anyway this just so happened to be the place where most of the Who related people were staying, surprise, surprise.

As it turned out it was fine, they all knew the situation, she was known. But so am I so it was cool.

The point to all of this being, towards the end of the evening, last call, I was introduced by Pete's brother Simon Townshend to his wife Janey who had just come in from London.

She said hadn't I been the English girl, Keith's girlfriend, at Ramport. " Skinny Georgiana with the bobbed hair?", is how she put it.

Yes, that was I. Well, she soon refreshed my memory and blew my mind in one fell swoop.

Back when we were in the midst of recording *Quadrophenia*, there were always the neighbourhood kids around. I was up at the Butcher's Arms, the pub up along Thessaly Road. All these kids wanted to get a chance to meet the Who, and as things would have it the guy who was doing the photographs for the book that was to accompany the album was on the lookout for kids to play the different parts.

As chance would have it, I took these few kids up to the studio and Pete thought they'd work for 'Jimmy' and the rest of the characters in the story line.

It just happens that one of the girls was a 14 year old Janey.

All these years later she tells me that from then on she and all her girlfriends used to hang around the studio, make cups of tea and so forth, I seem to remember it all vaguely. But what is so amazing to hear today is that I was a role model, their role model. They apparently used to try to dress and wear their make-up like me and so forth. This was so strange to hear. At 23 you don't reckon to be anybody's' idea of a trend-setter.

It turns out that from that incident she met Pete's brother Simon, and they now have been married about 30 years, have three kids, and all because of me, what a trip. I had been totally oblivious to this all these years. Strange how fate just put me in their path again to find all this out.

Me, Simon Townshend, Janey Townshend.

After the making of *Quadrophenia* I really can't think of anything in particular. Although I know things did happen, nothing just pops into my head off hand. No specific anecdotes.

There were numerous shows, lots of partying, craziness of one sort or another, but nothing I can put my finger on. Keith and I went to Tramp in Jermyn Street a lot. We would sit with Ringo, and Harry Nilsson, and Billy Laurie, among others, like John Conte, the boxer, and Dudley Moore and all and sundry that dropped by our table. Sometimes life just goes on like that for a while, with the same stuff going on night after night, in different combinations. then one day you realize a decade has passed

Chapter 8

Though there were many incidents I could recount they would have no rhyme or reason and just be isolated incidents and anecdotes with little relation to anything in particular. Though they may well crop up during the telling of this, be pertinent to the story and fit right in.

The Seventies do this a lot to me when I try and recount anything in particular. Tells something of the times doesn't it?

Things went on. Sometimes good and sometimes horrid. But that's what makes life interesting isn't it?

There were ordinary days and the out of the ordinary, like Keith deciding he and Dougall and I should eat Maltese food one night, so we flew to Malta. I still have only ever seen the airport the taxi and the restaurant, then back to the plane.

The movie of *Tommy* was made at Shepperton Studios around this time. Keith was busy during the filming and I spent more and more time running around London. Times were more free, people more understanding, and it was relatively safe.

Like any couple we had our ups and downs. Probably more so as we never really defined our relationship, people were less analytical of their lives then than they are now, with all this bonding and sharing and quality time new age vernacular of later times. We were together when we were together and when we weren't we were alone, or with someone else. The primary people in each other's lives were each other.

Whatever, it worked.

I had my foray's into intimate friendships with no particular meaning or emotion attached.

The times were just like that. *"If you can't be with the one you love, love the one you're with...."*

Actually this precedes the Keith Moon times anyway. These casual attachments.

One of these people I need to mention, as it fits into the small world department so well.

On my 20th birthday I met a guy called David Anthony, a photographer. We had both dropped Acid at the gathering at the flat in Cheyne Place and ended up at his place in Quex Road in Maida Vale. We weren't an item, though frequently ended up together, on and off through my being and not being with Keith, and David was always with some model or other, or his wife later on, but no matter.

The coincidence being, and why I'm mentioning this at all is that when I had met Gordon Waller in Los Angeles in 1966, Gordon and David were flat mates back in London. A house in Baker's Mews.

David Anthony & I in 1998.

David Anthony in 1972.

Life is full of those wheels within wheels, at least mine is, I don't know about yours.

I continued to travel down to Ibiza in the summer, and my stays got longer and longer.

There too I had a little romance, or just sex.

One really nice guy I always remember was Andreas. He was a blonde, Northern Spaniard with long, curly hair, rather like Roger D. I suppose the reason I remember him is not for his life, but the way his death made an impression on me.

One summer I flew into Ibiza. It's a small island, and when I was out in the open I noticed I could hear Elton John's *"Requiem For A Friend"* playing all over the island, it seemed.

The reason, the sad reason, I soon found out was that Andreas was being buried that day. He had been at a party and a puppy had fallen down the inside well of the finqua. Andreas had lowered himself down the rope only to have it break, he fell and I believe broke his neck. It's sad, but he deserved a mention I suppose.

One of my many friends who is unfortunately no longer with us.

Andreas' passing was somehow more noble than many of the others, but no better.

So there was Keith and David and Bo and Andreas and Gordon and even Mr...., but I shouldn't speak out of turn. Some people have lives and people in them since all that has happened. Some times are better left to private and personal memories.

The trouble is in trying to remember a lot of it! I'm discovering more and more, especially since starting this, that there are large chunks of my memory completely glossed over, or blocked out. Things that I did that should have stayed with me but didn't.

It's strange as I was only made to realize by this occurrence, just how altered I must have been by the lifestyle I was involved in at that time.

Mandrax, a form of methalquaalude, that was the Quaalude of America, was the memory snatcher of this period of my London life, that and good old brandy and dry ginger.

There was a place that became very popular in the early Seventies called the Rainbow. Not to be confused with The Rainbow Bar & Grill on the Sunset Strip. This Rainbow was a concert venue that had been an old movie palace of the 1920's, the Finsbury Park Astoria, in North London.

The Who opened it and top groups of the time played there week after week.

I could always remember going there quite a bit, but not to the extent I was reminded of while talking to my friend Michael Mitchell recently. He tells me we went there just about every week one year.

I know that I knew someone there, on the door, probably from being there at the opening with the Who. Because of that occurrence we could go there whenever we wanted, or rather whenever we showed up.

I do remember going to see Mountain, and Foreigner, and The Pink Floyd, not so much of seeing the shows, just of being at the venue.

The Rainbow, a circular sort of building rather like the Roundhouse which was an old railway roundhouse originally, had a series of rooms around its' outer perimeter, upstairs and down. They were dressing rooms, holding areas and bars and you could get lost, and spend inordinate amounts of time traversing these corridors as they always seemed filled with people partying. I'd be walking along, minding my own business, when suddenly someone I knew would call a "hello" and I'd stop and chat a while, have a drink or whatever, then go on my way only to run into someone else. By the time I'd make my way back into the auditorium the show would be over. Or I'd cross through the auditorium on my way to the other side of the building and catch a bit of a performance here and there. It was a unique situation to be sure. I am sure it wasn't peculiar just to me as all these other people I'd run into were there in the same capacity for the most part. Just hanging around.

One person in particular I remember who seemed to be there a lot was when I was also was the Scottish comedian Billy Connelly. Long before he became famous throughout the world. We'd sit at the bar and chat on occasion.

One funny chance meeting years later happened when I was working at Warner Brothers Studio in Burbank. I was wrapped and on my way off the lot when I noticed Billy's T.V. show, *"Saved By the Bell"*, , was taping so I went in, told a stage hand my name and asked him to please tell Billy that I'd like to say hello, not really thinking he'd remember me as it had been years.

I was really pleasantly surprised when he came right out of wherever he'd been and gave me a big hug and started talking a blue streak about this and that, asking if I'd seen Bobby Reid, Booby Daniels, etc. Other Scots we knew in common.

He obviously remembered a lot better than I did about those days around the Rainbow and its' environs. We reminisced and promised to keep in touch. But our paths have not really crossed since.

Chapter 9

The *Tommy* film was ready to be promoted and off we went to the States. Not en masse, but I ended up in L.A. in March of 1975. I stayed with my old friend Heidi in Venice Beach and we caught up on old times. We went to the Renaissance Faire when it was still out in one of it's original sites in Dekker Canyon, the now Paramount Ranch. I have being trying to remember if this particular visit was the last time I saw Heidi, or if I spoke with her on a subsequent visit the following year. No one remembers, and Heidi doesn't communicate with anyone she used to know for some reason only she is privy to as she now lives her new life in Tallahassee, Florida. All the best Heidi.

Heidi Friars & I, 1975.

I stayed in Venice and I also stayed with my other old friend Cathy Rowland and her boyfriend, later to be husband, Dennis, in Beverly Glen. I looked up old friends and made new ones and went to movie premiers that I didn't watch and parties afterward, and discovered The Rainbow Bar & Grill, which hadn't been going on the Strip when I had left in 1969.

I stayed a few months and then returned to London. I think that summer was the last I went to Ibiza. Franco had died and the King of Spain, Juan Carlos, was in. Not that it has anything to do with anything, or my going to Ibiza or not. It just stopped being on my agenda and I didn't notice.

Cathy Rowland, Georgia Rowland, me and Gail Murphy, 1975.

Times change, and we with them, now I realize it was the beginning of getting older, or more mature.

Life wasn't all just fun and games though. I did make an honest attempt at working. not so much to make money, or I didn't consciously think so at the time. I didn't particularly want for anything, I was always clothed, fed and housed. It was just for something to do.

Besides that sojourn into retail at Casa Pupo, I had and equally short stint at the ultra-trendy Biba's in Kensington High Street. This was interesting as they used their sales people as models and we had an assigned outfit to wear every day.

Unfortunately mine was a bright green crepe, thirties-style thing. The really unfortunate thing about it was they had everything in coordinated colours and I was required to wear matching eye-shadow, nail polish and lip-stick, all in the bright green shade of this dress. Really bad!

I had to ride the tube from Sloane Square every day and though it was only one stop to High Street Kensington, I must have made for an interesting sight made up like that. Actually I probably looked like most of the other people of my age in London at that time. Needless to say this job lasted about as long as the dress before it needed cleaning.

Just another sojourn into the pre-Who times.

Shortly after *Quadrophenia* was finished and show-cased, as it were, all over Britain, other bands started coming into Ramport. It was, after all a working recording studio and the Who weren't a studio band exclusively. I continued working there during a lot of these sessions, and came to meet John Alcock, who was producing various groups at this time. I believe I had met John earlier, through his being a friend of John Entwistles', also of Cyranos', another friend involved with the Who over the years. So, it came to pass that I started sitting in on the sessions and putting in my two cents, or tuppence as it were. John must have liked my opinions as I was soon co-coordinating/co-producing. This was very cool. Very good for the old self-esteem, also a new gig.

We recorded the Earl Slick Bands' *"Razor Sharp"*, Thin Lizzie's *"Johnny The Fox"* album, and a group from Scotland called Bandit. Then in November of 1976 we came out to Los Angeles, *"WE"* being John and myself and our engineer Will Reid-Dick, to ultimately go up to The Record Plant in Sausalito and record Commander Cody and His Lost Planet Airmen. *"Mid-Night Man"* album.

Although this was work it was really a study in lunacy of a sort. In fact I was talking to John about this time in our history together and it was again quite amazing, that we survived. Not this particular episode as it were, but the entire life-style we were all into. Just to be able to function working and playing to the extent that we did was quite a feat.

I came across some of the photos recently, and we didn't look at all well, but we did look like we were having a passably good time at it. Just to elaborate on the kinds of things we got up to I'll need to go back to the beginning of our association at Ramport.

Not all is really clear, but John reminded me of how, during one of the Earl Slick sessions Earl put John's extremely small car, known as The Roller-skate, into someone's front garden near Ramport one night. Lifted it right over the fence they did. Now this was an amusing little episode to say the least, but I still have a hard time trying to remember it. Shows how inured we all became to anything really absurd. Some things that should probably stand out in our memories as being really out of the ordinary, in all actuality became commonplace and so our thrills became more and more absurd. Downright dangerous as a matter of fact. That is probably why a lot of our contemporaries didn't survive, but not to get morbid.

There are a lot of similar instances, I'll try and relate them as I recall them, if I recall them. This is how all this got started. Every time I would tell a tale or anecdote of something in my past to others I would always get "You should write a book". So I have.

We got to L.A. In November of 1976. I came on a day or two ahead and stayed with another old friend, Gail. Gail began as Gail Waggoner, married a Widmer, and then married a Murphy, after the proper divorce procedures of course. Though no longer married to Brian Murphy, Murphy she remains, and my good friend she also remains.

So, Gail, Susie Trammel and I in Horseshoe Canyon, up Lookout Mountain in the famous Laurel Canyon.

Enter...oh so many people! Keith was staying at a house in Sherman Oaks, Knob Hill Road, I believe his Abba fixation in the persona of Annette Walter-Lax was around by then. But, no matter, back to all that later.

I spent Thanksgiving of 1976 up in Horseshoe Canyon, then when all that was over and we were down to turkey soup, John and Will arrived and the party began.

There was a steady stream of people either up at the house,or at John's hotel, which was the Chateau Marmont.

Sometimes we'd end up at one of the many places around town after the Rainbow. It seems, looking back on this time, that for people who were out there on a job that we had a lot of spare time on our hands before we actually had to go to work up North. Actually that is the way it is in all aspects of show-business in general, a lot of down time, idle time, time to get into mischief.

Will Reid-Dick, Gail, me, John Alcock and Cisco.
Record Plant, Sausalito, 1976.

Of course, there were details to be worked out with the record company and the studio and the band, etc. There was a quick trip to New York to get some front money from Clive Davis at Arista, and other such business. We went to Sausalito, at long last. By then we were all such close friends my friend Gail came along as well.

During the making of the album, George Frayne, Cody, The Commander, got married. We went on an adventurous journey to some hunting lodge way up north. It seemed at the time we drove for hours through fog and rain and enormous redwood trees to a log cabin in the Muir Woods.

George Frayne (Commander Cody) at his wedding.

It must have been a fairly good wedding reception as I can't remember it much at all. But, once again, I have photographs!

We drifted back to Los Angeles and went our own ways.

John and Will returned to London, I stayed in L.A., sort of continuing on from where I would have been had I not left in 1969, but with a lot of new experiences and friends and knowledge under my belt.

There was the Rainbow. A nightly event in those days for us, where everyone met to find out what everyone else was doing. Thereby finding out what they were going to be doing, and to be seen doing it!

I moved from the house in Horseshoe Canyon up the hill to watch a house belonging to John Mills, a boyfriend of Gails' while they were in Colorado.

John Mills was a recording engineer who lived at the top of Lookout Mountain in a house once owned by Cloris Leachman. John, along with John Arias produced and recorded Hall & Oates, as I recall.

It was a great house. All glass and wood.

Life went on in the night-life mode of sleeping late and getting ready to go out and then going out. Then usually going on somewhere afterward, going home and crashing. Or crashing and then going home!

I didn't have a car so I was pretty much at the mercy of whomever was driving. There was one guy, from London, by the name of Roger Charles who was selling cars. British cars, and who liked to party. We all drank and took drugs, cocaine mainly, but Roger tended to take things to the extreme at times, so I usually ended up driving his car. He had the new Triumph TR-3's a different one every night at one point. Before that he had MGB's.

There was no romantic involvement here I should say, just acquaintances really.

The point I'm making is that, being new in town and my knowing the way around and knowing people, I was assured of a ride, or at least a vehicle to drive practically every night, which was cool, except Roger usually brought some blow with him and then we'd go off and drink and I held my substances better, so one night as we fell out of The Rainbow I got the duty of driving and along about La Cienega and Holloway the Highway Patrol pulled me over, of course I failed the sobriety test and went directly to jail, without passing "GO" or collecting anything. Actually, it was the West Hollywood Sheriffs Station. I got out on my own recognizance the next morning.

The law wasn't as tough then and I got off with about a $270 fine and five years of summary probation.

I don't know what ever happened to Roger after that particular trip to America, but I wish him well.

The rest of this particular stay in L.A. was eventful to say the least. Lots of highs and lows.

After John and Gail returned from Colorado, I went a few houses down Lookout Mountain to stay at a girls house that I met through friends at the Rainbow.

Pat Enyart was a budding photographer of rock groups and I guess she drifted in the direction of my friends and I by way of getting photo opportunities. So I stayed in her living room while she bunked with a very loud guinea pig in her bedroom!

We went out to The Bow (as the Rainbow was fondly called) and to the record company bowling nights at the La Cienega Lanes.

I was still seeing an old boy friend from England, Bryan Rooney, at times and he bowled on the Monday night event. This was actually an excuse to drink, but I'll never tell.

Chapter 10

Bryan was a guy from Liverpool I had met years before in London, at the Speakeasy with Terry Doran, Mick Coles and the like. They worked at Apple, The Beatles company in Saville Row.

We were in company leagues even back then when I used to play on their darts team at various times in various pubs around London. He's always been a dear friend, he danced at my wedding with my sister-in-law! He was being house husband up in Saugas with his wife Jill and new daughter Gemma, and I was very saddened to learn from Booby recently that Byran passed away from cancer just before Christmas of 2006.

Back in 1976, in L.A. Bryan had worked for Ringo and I ran into him at Ringos' New Years Eve party at the house up on Sunset Plaza, which sadly burnt to the ground a number of years ago, along with a lot of Ringo's memorabilia.

Funnily enough Bryan was by then working for Keith Moon, driving Keith's Excalibur and living at the house in Victoria Point Road in the Malibu/Trancas area, next to Steve McQueen and Ali McGraw. Keith by then had Annette Walter-Lax there..

So, the usual and more of the same in the ensuing months. Pat moved to an unfurnished house way down in old Hollywood that summer and it was pretty grim. I had been hanging at the Bow as usual. Through some friends from London, Keith Robertson, who had worked for the Who when I did, and Bob Pope I met other mutual friends. Two of these guys, Alan Phillips and Bobby Reid helped change the course of my life was to take once again. Not that they changed my life, they just were there when the direction changed. They are definitely the only link I can think of as to the next segue of this part of my life.

Keith Robertson and Bobby Reid.

Alan was, and still is, a cheery guy from Wales, a songwriter who had worked at Apple and produced Colin Blunstone's album. He was very social, so it's probably through him that Pat and I started talking to them one night. I really can't remember the circumstances. He was with a quieter Scottish guy called Bobby Reid. Bobby wasn't so quiet really, kind of brooding is more like it. No matter. We all started hanging out together.

Alan Phillips, 1970s.

Bobby lived up in this great house on Mullholland Drive at Coldwater Canyon that had once belonged to Sabu the Elephant Boy, from the 30s adventure movies. He didn't have the place to himself though, this was rented by one Richie Leiber and his girlfriend Joyce, but I get way ahead of myself here.

Like I said, Alan, Pat, Bobby and I just started hanging out together, like people tended to do back then. We'd go up to Bobby's and just hang. We'd crash out in the same bed watching television. That kind of thing. Simple. Innocent. Like kids at a slumber party.

I don't recall how, when, where or why it came about that we paired off as it were, but eventually I ended up with Bobby. It wasn't just a one-night-stand thing. No, it was a while in happening and I ended up moving out of Pat's and into the house on Mullholland with Bobby.

Bobby was really nice, although he had his problems, like everybody, but it isn't necessary to go into to continue my story. Suffice it to say, he was on the outs with his brother John Reid, who managed Elton John and Queen at the time, through his Rocket Records label. Bobby had been working with John, but some sibling rivalry, and the fact that John is gay caused the rift. So, my first assumption of Bobby having a brooding personality was correct. All that and I seem to recall he was enamored of a girl in Orange County who just didn't want to know.

As I said before, Richie and Joyce rented this house. As you can imagine a huge place like this didn't come cheap, I think even in 1977 it was about $1500 a month. In retrospect this was cheap as dirt, in todays' money it would be around the $7000 to $10,000 per month mark I should think.

I soon found out the way Richie made the rent. There was a phenomenon back then called the Swing Party. This was where couples, sometimes singles, would pay $40 and bring a bottle to a designated party house and literally fuck all night. Orgies!

I had never come into contact with people who were into this. Obviously, in my world, the generation of free love, these occasions weren't necessary. It was really weird.

Bobby and I never got involved in these affairs, (excuse the pun). We usually went down to the Bow and when we got back it was all over with. There did come a time when Richie asked for help organizing these things, after all we were living there rent free, So we became involved in that capacity. I would take reservations over the phone during the week. He advertised in the L.A. Free Press, etc. So, I would take reservations as I sat around the pool that summer of 1977, then I'd cook the hot hors d'oveurs for the party, If we stayed, Bobby would check the reservations, and money at the door and I'd work behind the bar for a while.

It was really quite civilized up in the living room. It was only downstairs in the water bed room, or the mirrored room or the Jacuzzi room that things looked like a Roman orgy

Joyce always left, and Richie would either leave or just lock himself in his room till it was over.

It sure was weird, but hell, it paid the rent. Luckily there was no sign of AIDS back then.

Joyce used to go the Hugh Hefner's for his open-house up at the Playboy Mansion, and she invited me once. I had been up there with Keith and Dougall, this time was different.

They had a staffed, constantly supplied buffet and bar and people milling around. The Playboy types. Lounge suits and Bunny's.

I was really quite bored, but I was there to see the film, as they showed a first run movie on these Sunday's and I hadn't seen *"The Rocky Horror Picture Show"*. We watched the film and then Hef says something like, "O.K. All the girls down to the Grotto!" I really didn't want to be bait for his friends down in the Jacuzzi so I caught a cab out of there. Needless to say Joyce told me later that I wasn't to be invited back. Big deal. I doubt I would have gone back had I had an open invitation that the others seemed to have. It just wasn't my scene. Something to goof on is all. Life went on at the house on Mullholland. Bobby and I had the place pretty much to ourselves for the most part. We went to the Bow and hung around the house a lot as well.

My dad came out on business and we put him up in the mirror room and he thought it was really amusing waking up and seeing himself reflected in all the walls and ceiling!

I went with him on a business trip to San Francisco and we stayed at the Mikado. He was over in the States in the capacity of author and presenter of a booklet he had written about a charitable foundation for Gifted Children.

When we returned to L.A. he took a room at the Sunset Marquis.

One day he had got in touch with his old buddy John Carradine, the actor, and we were to meet John at the Cock & Bull restaurant on the Strip. We sat at the bar for a few before lunch cocktails, and as far as I recall we never did eat. John had the reputation of being able to put it away in fairly large quantities. He usually drank till he couldn't drink any more then would call two cabs. One for him and one so the driver could take his car to his destination for him, which was, at that time a room at the Hyatt House. This time however we all took a cab back to my dads' room at the Marquis, where Bobby was waiting as it turned out. John kept referring to him as "that sullen Scot".

After a few more drinks of my fathers' duty free Scotch a cab was called, perhaps it was two this time, and off John went to the Hyatt, or Riot house as we used to call it at that time. I suppose I should add that John lived in Montecito then so he couldn't exactly go home!

89

Bobby and I crashed in the other twin bed in the room. My dad was very cool. Bobby however felt strange about sleeping with me in the same bed in the same room with my father and I do believe the next time we ended up in a similar situation he and I took a room at the Hyatt House ourselves.

During that time I had a call from another old friend of my parents, and father of old friends of mine. Fred Phillips, father of Nina and Janna and he was also the brother of a guy my mum had dated way back in the 30s, Webster Phillips. Fred was a dear man who was a fabulous make-up artist. He had done the *"Twilight Zone"* and *"Outer Limits"* television series and the *Star Trek* series and movies. At that time he was doing the make-up and prosthetics for a series called *"The Man From Atlantis"*, with Patrick Duffy. He always kept in touch with me when I was in town and one day called to ask if I would like to come to the set with he and Janna, who was learning the trade from her father, and possibly work as a Extra on an episode of the show. Sure, why not.

I met him before dawn at his place one morning and we went to pick up a friend of his who was also to be a guest star on the show, the little person, Billy Barty, along with Billys' son and daughter. So off we went to San Pedro. It rained off and on and I was invited to stay in Billys' trailer rather than with the general population of Extras. Then there was an announcement that came over the P.A. system. Elvis Presley had died of an overdose in Memphis, Tennessee. There was total silence for what seemed like an eternity. It certainly always enables me to pinpoint where I was when I heard that news.

Sort of like when I was sittingagainst a handball court at Milliken Jr. High eating a sandwich and reading Shakespeare, another announcement came over the P.A. The President had been shot and classes were suspended for the day, so we were to go home. It was the 22nd November 1963. JFK died on a Friday.

Chapter 11

I got home that day in 1977 to the house on Mullholland and it was pouring rain and Richie announced that we had to move. There was some sort of upheaval I don't know what. If memory serves me at all I think Bobby and he had had a falling out and Bobby had actually gone to stay at Alan's apartment a week or so earlier. This was all really inconvenient, and quite frankly I didn't know where I was going to go.

I have a recollection of going to Alan's, but it was a temporary situation as he only had a one bedroom place and it wasn't possible for Bobby and I to both sleep on the sofa for long.

Soon thereafter I must have moved into Maria Perez' place, it suits the time frame if not the memory!

She was a very young friend of someone's, Bobby I think, only seventeen or so, but very mature for her age. Her mother was very liberated and paid for her to have a new car and a really nice place on the corner of Sweetzer and Fountain. Now that I am older I actually think liberation was not the real reason her Mom did this. But being divorced from her wealthy Dominican doctor husband she wanted her space and didn't need a teen-aged daughter around her and her new, younger boyfriend. But at the time, to someone in her twenties I just thought she was cool. I can attest to this fact from when they all came to London and hung out with me at J. Arthur's.

As this place on Sweetzer & Fountain had two bedrooms, I got one.

Bobby went to stay at a friend of his' place down on Olympic and La Cienega. Funnily enough it was a similar situation. I think the two girls were even friends, but her mother was widowed and wealthy and paid for Jill to have a place and a Porsche. Jill Tavelman knew most all of the bands that came through town. Her father had been the tailor to George Burns and that ilk and was much older than her mother.

Anyway, she was very sweet, and though I haven't seen her in years she did very well for herself and married Phil Collins, had his daughter and has since broken up with Phil and divorced, but I hear will be well provided for. Congratulations Jill. Little did I know that when you came to London and slept on my floor, that the guy you came to pick

91

me up with at the dentist one day was Phil and not a mini-cab driver! I really thought that's what he was till we stopped at Air recording studio in Oxford Street and he took off his cloth cap and started singing. He must have still been with Genesis then.

Jill Tavelman & I in London.

So, I was staying at Maria's and Bobby was over at Jill's. Sometimes I would stay over at Jill's as well.

I should say that sometime before we left the Mullholland house Bobby had approached me with a plan, a proposition as it were. We were down in the billiard room one night shooting pool when he asked if I thought I might like to get married. "For the Green Card", he quickly added. "Sure", I said. We had a plan.

Somehow it never really seemed serious, the marriage proposal I mean. Not that Bobby wasn't serious, I'm sure he meant it, at the time anyway. It was something to be filed away in the "things to do" file. As Bobby still was married to a woman in Scotland who had his children.

So, we went about our day-to-day business. I worked in the Publishing/Copyright department of Casablanca Records on Sunset for a while, when Neil Bogart died it all changed hands or closed down., more likely.

Maria worked at a small boutique across the street. We went to the Bow nightly and invariably had a bunch of people there afterward. This time strikes me as being a marching in place kind of existence. Nothing really exciting stands out, pretty humdrum really. Not that nothing at all went on. There were concerts that came through town, and the parties that went with them. Led Zeppelin were around, this was what was soon to be one of the last appearances of either Keith Moon or John Bonham around Hollywood. Ironically enough, one night at the Beverly Hilton, in Bonzo's suite, after a night of hard drinking and drug taking that Bonzo (jokingly, we think) called an ambulance to remove a very stoned Keith Moon from his room. I went on to the Forum in Bonzo's limousine and caught up with Keith later at the Rainbow. Little did anyone know at the time that Bonzo would be dead in a few months, followed closely by Keith in September of 1978. But we could all laugh at our antics then.

Came the Fall, and things started to wind down even further, and so it came to pass while hanging around waiting for Bobby and his friend Louie to come back to the room I was waiting in at the old Tropicana Motel on Santa Monica Blvd., that I rang the airlines and made a reservation for the open-ended ticket I had been hanging onto all year. I then phoned my parents to tell them I'd be flying back with Bobby Reid 20th October 1977. You see, once I knew Bobby had a flight number it was easier to pick a date.

Now that I had a direction things started to pick up socially, as they always do when you're just in town for a while.

One night at the Bow, Keith and I saw each other across a crowded room and the song goes, I can't recall the conversation, but time was short.

So, came October and I boarded the TWA flight that was to take Bobby and I to a new life, or so I thought.

From the time Bobby asked me to marry him there had been a distinct cooling trend, which I of course would not accept.

So pursue I did, as was my wont, which was a really bad habit of mine where relationships were concerned.

I don't think Bobby was really pleased to find me on the same flight as he and his buddy Louie. They were going over to England working for Davey Johnston and his band China's tour. Though I had my room at my parents flat I went along to the Holiday Inn, Marble Arch and hung around the room, I guess Bobby was politely tolerating my presence, I mean he wasn't rude or anything, just not as warm as he had once been. I soon found out this was because some girl he had met in Chicago when he was working with Elton John was showing up in London. This was indeed a drag, but I took it like a man and went to the bar and got very drunk!

While sitting in the bar feeling pretty much of nothing, except very sorry for myself, who do I see through the dim haze but a grinning face, missing a front tooth, but my dear friend Bryan Rooney.

He was also there, with some band or another, it must have been when he was working with Donna Summer, and staying in the same hotel for a day or two more before returning to L.A., so I moved down a floor, got my bearings and my self-esteem back and went home a few days later.

One day the doorbell rings as my parents and I are sitting down to dinner and lo and behold it's Keith (Moon). He is just as surprised to see me as I am to see him, we both last saw each other at the Rainbow in L.A., no word then as to our impending departures back to London, but there we were once again. The purpose of his visit was to introduce his new driver, John, to my parents. Keith had a tremendous respect and love for my parents. I know the feeling was mutual. They even shared the 23rd of August as a special day. Keith's birthday and my parents wedding anniversary. Keith sat and told of how he was turning his life around and getting off the booze, etc. and going into films, like Ringo had been doing. Oh, he had great plans, we were all so happy he had seen the light, as it were.

Christmas came and went, and the New Year was heralded in to no great fanfare that I can recall. 1978 was an extension of 1977 and I can think of nothing in particular in that time frame at all, not till the autumn anyway.

So came the summer and autumn and I was still moping around about Bobby, making Trans-Atlantic calls at night after the pub to a mildly friendly ex-fiancée'.

There were diversions, had to have those diversions.

Every year Paul McCartney had a party for Buddy Holly, Buddy never came, as he had been dead since 1959, very funny! The point is that when the *"Buddy Holly Story"* starring Gary Busey came out there was a premier and although Keith was living with Annette then, we were still very close, so I was invited. I can't go into the exact sequence of events, it just wouldn't be right, but the events of that night would surely change the course of a lot of lives. So, the movie, and the party and the inevitable going onto somewhere else, but I didn't feel right going on to where Keith and Annette were staying, plus I didn't care for the flat. It now belonged to Harry Nilsson, though it was the same flat that Mama Cass had died in some years earlier. I just didn't care to go.

It was later that same day, the party having carried on till the dawn, that my dad and I were at the Duke of Wellington when a telephone call came through. Thinking it was probably my mum I sent my dad to get it. He came back around the bar, he ordered me a large brandy and dry and told me to down it. The call had been from Kitty Moon, Keith's mother, she had called the flat and my mother had given her the number I guess. Keith had passed away that 7th September 1978, just a week after his 31st birthday.

I finished that brandy, and a few others, went home, played the track *"Bellboy"* off the *Quadrophenia* album and broke the record in two.

All the calls and the confusion and, well, enough said.

Keith was buried, I miss him, his family misses him, his mates miss him, we all miss him like hell, I for one am sort of mad at him for dying.

The causes, why's and where fore's surrounding his death have all been stated officially, And un-officially. And Keith, it has been seen to.

Thanks for the memories Keith, we love you.

Keith Moon

Chapter 12

Life went on, as it always does. I seemed to drift away from all the people I'd been around so long with Keith and the Who. It wasn't until the 20th reunion tour that I really made contact with anyone from that part of my life again. I don't know why that is either. I got the impression though that when we were all together again it was a first for everyone involved. I don't mean to say the other band members had lost touch with each other, or those close in the management capacity, and so on. It was the extended family that had drifted away.

This is how it happened.

I had only been slightly aware that the Who were even coming to L.A. to play at the Coliseum. I had an idea I'd like to go, but just never put any effort into it. It was weird, the will to re-enter that whole scene just wasn't there for some reason. It was almost as though I felt I wasn't a part of that world anymore, or that it was still kind of painful to see anyone associated with those happier times when Keith was around. It was a mis-guided feeling whatever it was. This was August of 1989.

It so happened that my friend Cathy and Georgia Rowland's father, George, had passed away that same week in August. I had not heard from them in a while so when Cathy called to tell me I was of course saddened as I had known her father since I was about nine years old. Having lost my own father only two years previously, in February 1987. I could imagine what she was going through only too well.

I went to the funeral and when I got home I heard on the radio about the Who show at the Coliseum. It wasn't my first knowledge of it however, as a few days before I had gotten a call from Phil Spector's secretary, Phil had asked her to call me to try and get tickets.

Fortified by a few glasses of wine after the funeral, I was emboldened to take off for the Coliseum. The show had already begun, so I walked up to the back gate and when approached by someone or other, I just asked if Bobby Pridden was around, mentioned I had worked for the band for years and I was allowed in. It just so happened that Bobby Pridden (the sound man) was just coming off a break and got me a pass, so I was in.

It just goes to show that you are meant to be where you are meant to be. Or, just good timing.

I wandered around seeing the show for the first time without Keith, Kenny Jones from the Faces was drumming for them, and I was noticing the differences and the similarities and feeling at home again.

What had I been thinking? That my tenure with the Who had come to an end because Keith had left the picture? No way.

After the show there was a party in a series of tents behind the Coliseum. Walking in there was a bit like walking into the Speakeasy in London. There was Cy and Wiggie and Paul and Adrian Gurvitz (although brothers Paul had changed his surname to Curtis). Then the trailer doors opened and first came Pete. He spotted me and his face cracked into a big surprised grin as he broke into his long-striding walk over to me, picked me up off the ground and spun me around. Then came Roger, he was a little more subdued than Peter, Heather was there so it was sort of understandable, though not necessary, we chatted away though.

Unfortunately the Ox, Mr. Entwistle had already departed for the Rainbow, so it was another three years before I was to see John again.

John Entwistle and I.

I realized how long it had been when I was re-introduced to a tall girl, the spitting image of Keith as a teen-ager. His daughter Mandy,

98

who had been a little girl of ten or so when her father had died was now 21.

I had had another strange encounter some years before this while working as an extra on *"St. Elsewhere"* at an hotel in Universal City. We were sitting around a table in one of the dining rooms when I heard an English voice I somehow recognized.

I said something like "Is that Kim? 'Used to live at Tara? Your Mother is Joan and your daughter Mandy?" To which she said "Is that Georgiana?" Kim and I saw each other frequently during 1987-1989 on various sets. Then she and her husband Ian McGloughlin, of the Faces moved to Austin, Texas and had a skin care busines. Just recently Kim was killed in a road crash down there. So sad and unnecessary.

I next saw Pete and John when Pete was touring with his rock opera *Psycho-Derelict*. There again I just marched myself off to the Wiltern Theater after having little joy on the telephone. There I ran into Ringo with his son Zac and his daughter, those name I forget, at the Will Call window. Then I heard a walkie-talkie backstage, and who should answer but Mick Hinton, one of the road crew whom I used to see daily at Ramport. Though I remembered the name I couldn't place him till I saw him. He however, I am happy to say, recognized my name immediately and had me come around the back and let me in. I hope Ringo found his seats.

After the show, back in the dressing room I again saw Bobby Pridden and Cy, Pete, much more subdued than at the Coliseum a few years before. John was mellow and quiet. I tended to think that he was a bit melancholy, out of all the rest he used to hang around with Keith and I the most. Perhaps he felt the loss a bit more on a personal level too. We now all miss him as well. Gordon & I just missed him, we went to Vegas to see the beginning of the Who tour a few years ago and when we got there I phoned over to the Hard Rock to tell John we were there, only to be informed he had just been found dead in his bed!

Chapter 13

Back to 1978.

I was still half-heartedly pursuing Bobby. Not so much because I still wanted him but I didn't like being dumped. Also, there wasn't much else to do.

I contacted Alan Phillips again, and Booby. Booby and his girlfriend lived way up in North London somewhere and when I went to visit and would hang there for a few days. One night we were to meet at La Chasse in Wardour Street. This was a musician's bar, next door and upstairs from the Marquis Club, one of the places the Who played when they first started. As the High Numbers, or perhaps the Detours.

Off I went. I believe I met them there. We did all the usual. Drinking Pina Colada's if I remember correctly, talking and listening to music.

When it came time to leave, probably about 4:30 am, I was flagging down a black, London cab when Frank Coe, the owner/manager of the Chasse and the girl he was with said I should save on cab fare by sharing their mini-cab, as they were going through Fulham to the West.

We all piled in and I recall asking to stop on the way, in Piccadilly Circus to get a packet of cigarettes. Getting back into the back seat on the opposite side to where I had been before. Frank was up front next to the driver, and his friend Christine was now on my left.

The Pina Colada's had been strong and I dozed off, this was probably a life-saver, literally, in fact smoking and drinking proved beneficial to my health that night.

The next thing I remember was waking up in a bright room, flat on my back with my father looking down at me with a very pained expression on his face.

It seems somewhere along our journey we had been broad-sided by a van, big time.

I mean, I was later to find out we had rolled a number of times and had been freed by the jaws-of-life.

Frank had broken his legs rather badly, the girl Christine was in a coma, I had injuries to my head, severing the fifth nerve in my forehead and losing feeling in the left side of my head and face for some four to five years hence. I had broken my front teeth off, and with various other nicks, scrapes and cuts I was definitely not a pretty sight. No wonder my poor father had a dismal look about him. Along about the next night, the accident having taken place on the 13th/14th November 1978, so on the morning of the 16th, I awoke in my bed at the then St. Stephen's Hospital in the Fulham Road, with an awful belly-ache. I thought I just needed a bed pan, but when I started expanding around the middle it appeared that my spleen had not only ruptured but exploded! I was surrounded by nurses and no one was telling me what was going on. I recall asking a little West Indian nurse if I was going to die, to which she replied, "Oh, we no 'sposed to tell patients dese tings", to which I said something to the effect that it was my fucking life and I wanted to know! She responded that my spleen had ruptured and "...if we don't find a surgeon you have about 20 minutes, you got no messages for no one?"

This had a really weird effect. I became very calm and practical, of course my blood-pressure was down to nothing, I don't recall that I had any messages except to find a surgeon and for him to do a good and neat job.

So, I lived. The surgeon did a good job I 'spose! I thank that little West Indian girl for telling me the truth, wherever she may be.

I was in the hospital for a few weeks. Thank God for the National Health. My recovery took some time, but not as long as poor Christine, who when I last heard was still in a coma. I didn't really know her at all, having just met her when we left the club that fateful night. I had to go back to the hospital some months later to see if I would recognize her.

I didn't.

I always think what might have happened if I hadn't gotten out of that side of the cab in Piccadilly Circus for cigarettes, out of the impact side.

Whatever. My destiny didn't include that scenario just yet, I hope it never will.

There was that eerie feeling of having lost Keith a month or so earlier, he always liked to have me around and...well I know it's silly, but these things do go through an idle mind once in a while.

Things slowly regained composure and perspective and I had a small settlement, which all took an extraordinarily long time and it seemed all I wanted to do was return to Los Angeles. It took another four years of total inactivity.

I went through a lot of physical therapy and a lot of brandy and ginger, and a lot of library books. I'd go to the pub and drink, and sometimes go onto Tramp, Morton's, Legends, the Village, to play Blackjack or the Playboy Club to shoot Craps. Then I'd come home, and if I didn't just pass out I'd read till dawn, sleep till dusk and start all over again. A nowhere kind of existence really.

There were other clubs and I'll give them all honourable mention later.

I'd been to Morton's, in Berkeley Square one night, and when I returned and was getting ready for bed, I had the radio on, and suddenly the innocence went out of life. John Lennon had been shot and killed on the streets of New York, in front of his Dakota Apartment building.

Everyone on the streets of London, and I should imagine on the streets of other cities of the world, looked as though they had just lost their best friend. And they had.

Yes, things did indeed begin to change. We were coming of age, or coming into the realization of what age, and the passage of time brings. A sense of our own mortality.

There had, so far, been the Viet Nam war, where many of our age were lost, and not only through death. Then on personal levels there were many lost, and not only through death but through the excesses of our youthful follies. There were Jimi and Janis. I had personally lost Keith and other friends, Russell Gilbert, Neil Rappaport to name but two. Then there was poor Diane Horton in Camarillo State mental hospital, who died shortly after her release. Bobby Jamieson had jumped from the Pacific Theatre tower on Hollywood and Cahuenga Blvds. He survived and became one of the proponents and premier advocates for sobriety in AA. Though not right away. Then there was John Lennon, one of the cornerstones of the reason we all embarked on this journey in the first place. This culture of peace, love, and music in the early Sixties.

Arthur Lee and Jimi Hendrix, upstairs at the Whiskey.

Yes the world was indeed changing, and none of us who saw what was happening wanted it to. Not in the way it was going anyway. Progressive change is good. There was the death and destruction of an ideal that had sounded so good, and seemed to work quite well in the early stages. Of course the drugs ultimately didn't work (or they worked too well) The free love worked only for a summer or so, the rest of it, well it should have prevented the wars and the violence. The peace and love and caring for one another should have prevented the overdoses and the killing of our friends and icons. And with the advocate of *"All You Need Is Love"*.

With age comes the realization that no matter what innovations we have brought to the world nothing lives forever. We are not invulnerable. I see now that each and every generation thinks this. We do some pretty foolhardy things in our extreme youth, nothing can hurt us it seems, simply because we are young. Then, as we get older we slow down. Hey, we could get hurt doing that! Of course, some never slow down. Eventually, they are just stopped.

My personal caution started when that West Indian nurse told me I had about 20 minutes to live. It's like the old joke of death being natures way of telling you to slow down. I often think that a few of the one's we lost might still be around if they had had a near miss, instead of their final stoppages.

I also tend to think my wild and crazy days had an effect on my parents as well. Not long after my brush with eternity my dad had a slight stroke. He too recovered, but things weren't the same with his invulnerability either. Some of us carry the follies and habits of our youth well into our senior years I guess, which is cool, but awfully hard on the old body. The drinking and occasional smoking had to take a back seat, and though he fought it as long as he could, still taking his afternoon pints and evening whiskey's the doctors won out and it was Perrier or something as innocuous on visits to the pubs and clubs for the rest of his life.

Finally, in 1981, with a legal settlement near, but not finalized, my solicitor fronted me the money to buy a plane ticket to L.A.

I think I had made everyone's life thoroughly miserable by acting so down and miserable myself that the consensus was that it would be better to just let me go. I had held a torch for Bobby Reid all this time. It was all over but the shouting, but I held on to it anyway with the tenacity of a Pit Bull. I'd get drunk and phone him and send him the sports pages of the British newspapers to let him know what was going on with the soccer. Also, it was a way to send Mandrax rolled up in the pages. I had a doctor in London (didn't a lot of us) who prescribed 30 Mandrax and 30 ten milligram Valium every fortnight without fail.

So, the 22nd March 1981 came. I packed a few things, leaving the bulk of my life's possessions in my room in London and boarded the airport bus from Victoria Coach Station to Heathrow where I transferred to a trans-polar route TWA 747.

I won't say never to look back, but seldom.

That is until I started writing this.

At this point in my writing it has been exactly 14 years and two days since I landed at LAX. there have been many journeys within journeys since, and I hope, I know, there will be many more. I am now on the point of going back to London for a short visit. I have absolutely no idea what I will find there. I packed lightly when I left. I'm going to visit all my stuff. That and a few people and places my memory has recently dredged up. It should prove very interesting. I hope so anyway.

Chapter 14

During the course of this narrative I know I've mentioned various clubs and meeting places that certain events took place in.

Where would we be without the hot spots.

Or should I say where would these so-called hot spots be without us?

It's gratifying, on a certain level, to know that you were part of a group,, or culture that put a certain place on the map, so-to-speak.

It wasn't just the trendy nightclubs, with a line or two in the Rock anthologies that I speak of here. There were the hang outs and restaurants and coffee shops where things of great pitch and moment also took place.

My parents had always been great nightclub people in the hey day of Hollywood, going to the Trocodero, Mocambo and Ciro's. I guess it sort of rubbed off on me. Some of the clubs that had been famous meeting places of the stars of the 30s and 40s were still in business in the 60s. These, like Ciro's were adopted be the new wave of young club goers, or should I say taken over.

The earliest I recall clearly is Heidi and I talking her mother Betty into dropping us off, one Halloween, at The Fifth Estate on Sunset. This was a left-over of the Beatnik generation/Folk coffee house. Dylan, Baez, Alan Ginsberg, they would all frequent it when out from Greenwich Village, or so we were told, and sometimes saw for ourselves. All I recall is espresso, hot cider, poetry readings and folk music. It was 1965. I think we had fun.

The other club at that end of Sunset was Pandora's Box, on the island at Crescent Heights, but I think you needed ID to get in so a lot of people would just hang around outside. It was actually sort of shunned by a lot of us locals. More for the tourists and out-of-towners. I remember once Tina Turner was playing there and we didn't go because it wasn't one of our hip places! I went in a few times, but it was always crowded and dark and unfamiliar, so I don't recall a lot about it. It wasn't very comfortable and so I went to Bido Lido's and

The Brave New World, not that these were necessarily more comfortable but I think more of the people I knew went there.

These were both up in old Hollywood. Bido Lido's was on Cosmo & Selma, The Brave New World was on Melrose.

It was at Bido Lido's that the group Love first played, or first came to my attention anyway.

There were new friends made out of these sojourns. Neil Rappaport was a friend of Arthur Lee's and would sit in sometimes and play the harmonica. Neil was always sweet to us kids. He was a heroin addict but in the nicest way possible. Heidi and I used to go over to whatever cheap rooms he was living in at the time and watch him eat junk food, most notably Twinkie's or Hostess Cupcakes, and watch him nod. This was, for some reason fun for a couple of fifteen year olds. He kept his habits to himself and we weren't curious about the high he was always behind, he was just nice I guess. He died sometime in 1968.

Heidi and I had just returned from the San Jose music festival to the house we were watching, along with the cougar Toy, in Livingston Way in Laurel Canyon, and Neil's brother Kenny, had phoned my mother to tell her about Neil's death,she then told us. It was a drag, but that is the risk with that lifestyle. There were a lot of accusations flying around that he had been given a hot shot (bad or poison dope) by someone we all knew, but it was never confirmed so I won't mention any names, those who were around know what the situation was. Like the situation surrounding Lenny Bruce's death.

Then there was Jeffie Eisen. Jiffy Jeffie. He always had a bunch of people around him and was very entertaining. What can I say? You had to be there.

Jeffie was a speed-freak, as those involved with methedrine were fondly called. I dabbled in the experience from time to time as well. I hung with Mark Rainsley, a talented artist, for a while. The others around that scene were Alan Dahlbeck, a dead-ringer for Richard Widmark, in fact he used to say he was his illegitimate son, and Jerry L'Etoile.

There were a lot of others who frequented the inner sanctums that were Bido Lido's and the Brave New World, but like I say, you had to be there.

Jeffie had a great dog called Tundra. Tundra was a white German Shepherd. We used to see Tundra, on his own frequently, no dog catcher's back then it seems. He'd hang in front of the Sun Bee Market on Sunset and if you called to him as you drove by it always looked like he looked up and smiled.

"Jiffy" Jeffie Eisen

There was an old Polish sculptor and his young wife at that time. Vito and Susie Polakowski. They had a following of freaks who would go around en masse and dance at the various clubs, not as hired dancers, but let in free to dance as customers, as ambiance I guess. So,

107

if you got to go in with Vito's Freaks, as they were known, well, I guess you were in with the in crowd!

Heidi and I would trail along sometimes. These were truly odd people. They were all much older than everybody else. There were Beatle Bob and Susie, Philippe', Karl Franzoni, who held the distinction of being able to touch his nose with his tongue, long before Gene Simmons of Kiss got known for that feat. Flo, who wore a string of safety pins in her ears long before the Punks were even born. I recall her other claim to notoriety was being a particular friend of Mick Jagger's on the Stones first tour to L.A. In 1965. Tommy Randall, and more whose names escape me now. I recall David Crosby and Mike Clarke stayed in Vito's loft for a time way early on in their careers with the Byrds.

David Crosby & I on the set of Roseanne.

This whole trip of Vito's came to ill when he and Susie's little baby, Godot, fell through the sky-light at their studio on Beverly and Laurel, and died. I've since heard that they were not very wholesome where it came to children, but I'd rather not get into this at all.

Vito was in his 60's then, I think I heard they went to Haiti, some were a little too friendly with the natives and died of AIDS, but you never know....

Chapter 15

Of course, other members of Love were also among the friends and acquaintances. There was Johnnie Echols, Brian MacLean, Kenny Forsee and Snoopy Pfister. There were a bunch of us who would sit on the wall in front of Hamburger Hamlet, which at that time was on the corner or Sunset and Hilldale. Arthur wrote a song that Love recorded called *"Between Clark & Hilldale"*, which I guess attests to this fact.

Starting at Clark, you had the Whiskey A'GoGo, next to the Whiskey was The Galaxy (also it was Sneaky Pete's, The London Fog it was an after-hours club called the Roulette Room for a time as well). As the Galaxy and The London Fog this is where the Doors and the Iron Butterfly first played. Then came the Bistro Beef 'n' Beer, with killer ginger-bread with whipped cream, then there was a book store/head shop called Sunset books where Michael Mitchell worked for a spell. Then Hamburger Hamlet. Anyway the Hamlet was somewhere people just gravitated and hung out, met and figured out where to go from there.

I don't know what everybody's fascination with walls was, but now that I think of it there was also the wall in front of the coffee shop Ben Frank's, and the wall/railing in front of the Canyon Country Store in Laurel Canyon. I guess it was something to sit on! In pre-pager society these are where you could go if you were looking for someone in particular. If they weren't there someone probably was who had seen them recently. It was a casual sort of information highway, on the highway. Starbuck's must serve a similar purpose today.

Then across from the mini-Strip on Sunset there was The Eating Affair.

This was in the mid-Sixties.

The songs I remember being played a lot on the juke-box there were the Stones' *"Let's Spend the Night Together"*, and the Four tops *"Bernadette"*. So that was what? 1966-67? A burger and fries place out of a darker Happy Days. The people in and out of there were some of the aforementioned and new ones. Miles Cilletti, who did my first

Astrological chart, (later on Heidi and I attended Carroll Righter's Astrology school, I still do some charts for friends today, but now I can use a computer) and Pete Hendleman, he was a cook there for a while, he along with Roger Varon, Cooker and Baby John also had a band and worked later at the clothing store Head East. Across from The Sea Witch, now North Beach Leather, where I recall seeing Chad and Jeremy one night. I worked at Head East briefly with these characters. Pete Hendleman was a fave of mine, despite him nodding off once on his feet, falling over and breaking all his front teeth off!

Ben Frank's, now gone and turned into a Mel's Drive-In had a wall that looked out on the Trip, formally the Tiger's Tail, and I believe before that in the Hollywood of the 30s and 40s The Mocambo.

I think the first artist I remember that performed at the Trip was Donovan. Possibly his first venue in Los Angeles. I can remember sitting there, and there were all these enlarged photos as panels along the walls of the popular people and rock stars of the day. When some really straight looking guy leaned over from his table and said "Hello Marianne" he then pointed to the photo of Marianne Faithful, it wasn't anything really, but it has stuck in my mind all these years, every time I think of the Trip.

One night, after seeing Donovan there, a bunch of us were up at Jeffie's on Woodrow Wilson Drive. I guess we were tripping, I mean I know we had dropped Acid, I think Donovan was experiencing his first trip that night. We were all sitting on the floor in a bedroom, passing joints, Donovan was playing a guitar and singing sometimes, he wrote a song while sitting there about everyone living on a big polka-dot, and this was weird, just as I was thinking that it never got any lighter out (who wore watches then) Jeffie jumped up onto the bed and pulled back the curtains to reveal tin foil covered windows. Once again, you had to be there.

Jeffie had a room-mate called Chinaman, very old China looking with the drooping long thin mustache and the long braid, a'la Fu Manchu. Very decorative.

Years later I tripped Donovan out. He had purchased the home belonging to the parents of friends of mine in England and gave a house-warming party. He had just married Linda, the ex girlfriend of Brian Jones. Anyway, he was surrounded by his guests in a large room playing and singing, asking for requests when I suddenly blurted out

"We're All Living on, a Big Polka-Dot" he went silent for a minute and then said "Jeffie?" It was all he needed to say.

The clubs then had some fantastic bills now that I think back on it. Of course they were just the bands of the day so it was obvious that they should be playing in the local clubs. Who knew they would become legends?

In a typical week at the Whiskey for instance I can remember seeing Cream, Hendrix, and the Animals.

The Byrds started out at Ciro's, Dylan showed up at their first gig, to hear how they covered *"Mr Tambourine Man"* he got up and sat in with them.

Roger McGuinn at Ciro's in 1965, when he was still Jim.

Like I said before, the Doors and the Iron Butterfly played at the Galaxy, (as it was becoming the London Fog) almost un-noticed. There were acts in those days at Gazzari's I didn't go in there much. If I remember correctly it seems that both Gazzari's and Pandora's Box catered to the tourists more than the locals in the long run. I could be wrong, but that is my impression now looking back on it all.

Bob Dylan, 1965.

There was the Cheetah, but it was way out at the beach in Santa Monica, and it was a larger venue. The Byrds played there and Big Brother, I think as well. A lot of the bigger groups of the day. Out that way was also The Topanga Corral, Hendrix actually played there way before he became known.

The Shrine had a weekly dance thing at the hall next door to the auditorium. The Bryds and the Grassroots, the Seeds were there frequently.

We'd all head out there, usually with Vito's people, and of course get in free and dance the night away.

At the Shrine.

All in all the club scene in L.A. was great in those days. Always something going on. Of course, because seeing these great acts became quite commonplace, I guess we didn't give them the attention we would today had we the chance. Imagine leaving in the middle of a Hendrix set today, after all you could catch the next set, or the next day even. Sure!

Chapter 16

As always, things began to change. Just subtly at first, but change they do. I don't recall the first to go, but one by one the clubs either changed formats or closed down altogether. Of course, the bands became too big to stick to these small venues around town, so who was going to fill in that could compare with what had been? The age of large stadiums and the 'Glam-Rock' era was fast approaching, drawing the name acts away from the small clubs.

The Trip just sort of fades out from my memory. One day it just wasn't there anymore. Ciro's turned into the Kaleidoscope, with Pop Art comic book characters on the walls, then it became The Comedy Store. Which it still is today. I went there with a group of friends, Stephen Stills and some of his crowd, to see Richard Pryor. Richard never showed up so Robin Williams, in the audience to see the elusive Mr. Pryor, got up and did over an hours set.

Modeling gig for Seventeen magazine at The Kaleidoscope.

The Brave New World and Bido Lido's were among the first to disappear. All the clubs seemed to move westward. The Cheetah closed down, I know not why, probably due to lack of interest. It was a little too far west. Pandora's Box was closed soon after the riot on the Strip and the whole topography of the street changed as the island was torn down to widen the intersection there. The old Fifth Estate now has a statue of Bullwinkle Moose in front of it!

The Galaxy became Sneaky Pete's, The London Fog, then an after hours place, it is now Duke's Coffee Shop. The Whiskey went through many incarnations, almost burnt down in the early Seventies, went Punk for a while, and funnily enough has almost come full circle and has some of the original acts, the one's that have survived anyway. Every July 3rd, on the anniversary of Jim Morrison's death, a group that has cloned them, Wild Childe, would play at the Whiskey and they had Arthur Lee and Love on the bill the first couple of years.

Gazzaris' continued on till Bill Gazzari's death in 1994. It is now something called The Billboard Club. Something to do with Billboard magazine I should imagine.

The Palomino Club in North Hollywood finally closed down recently after decades there on Lankershim. Toward the end they were booking acts like The Strawberry Alarm Clock and Love.

There have been other places come and go. Bars mostly, no live acts to fill the bills I guess. Oh, the seedier clubs along the Boulevard, like Raji's have alternative, but as the music changes so do the venues.

There is also the Coconut Teazer, it used to be Frascatti's, where my father would take me to sit on the terrace and drink Shirley Temples on John Forsythe's lap, they showcased bands nightly, but recently have hoarding around the building once more.

All the great ones are gone.. I'm just really glad I was around for the start of it all, and that I was still around at the end.

There were a few other attempts at large clubs in L.A. There was The Factory. It rented itself out to private functions after a brief popularity, then I believe it turned into a gay club.

There were the bar/restaurants of the Seventies. The Beverly Hills trendy spots, all really boring to me. Like Pips, the Candy Store, and Nick's Fish Market. La Dome in the Eighties.

The unincorporated portion of Los Angeles, known as The Sunset Strip, is still the most popular portion for clubs. The County has never been as strict as the L.A.P.D. And so, since the 1920's has been the preferred place for nightclubs, through prohibition and gambling, all much more lenient than other incorporated sections of the city.

The only one that really caught on was The Rainbow. There's still The Roxy, they get name acts, but recently have catered to the Punk crowds, on mostly a 'pay-to-play' format. With so much Indie stuff going on now, big labels don't have the big show-casing parties of the past so much. Bands who want exposure must pay the clubs to see their names up on the marquee. That, or guarantee a certain amount of ticket sales. The Roxy has a concert style setting, not a dance club, or concert seating, just a bunch of tables scattered around, though there is a dance floor, it was just filled with standing kids the last time I went to see a band showcased there. There's still the private drinking club On The Rox upstairs, but I shouldn't think the likes of Keith's contemporaries frequent it anymore, Lou Adler and Britt Eckland were the patrons last time I was up there.

I imagine the Lingerie Club is still going way up on Wilcox and Sunset, I saw Love play there 3 or 4 years ago. The Cat & Fiddle, a British pub owned by Kim Gardner of Ashton,Gardner & Dyke is up that way. Kim died of lung cancer a few years ago and it is now run by his widow, Paula. There is also the Hollywood Billiard Club in the same area.

There was always Filthy McNasty's, a more adult bar over on Sunset and Larrabee. this became The Central in the mid to late Seventies and through the Eighties was quite the hang-out, before becoming The Viper Room.

When I first returned to L.A. in 1981 I was there and The Rainbow just about every night. They had a Jam Night every Tuesday and whoever was in town seemed to come in to play with the house band Jack Mack and the Heart-Attack. John Belushi used to come in and play drums, in fact he played there on the night of his demise later at The Chateau Marmont.

Another adult-oriented bar was The Classic Cat. This was where Tower Video now stands across Larrabee from what was once The Central. Now the Central is Johnny Depps ultra-trendy, exclusive night spot The Viper Room. This is where that poor (stupid) kid River Phoenix made his exit from out in front of. On the same mixture of drugs that took Belushi out, and even more recently the comedian Chris Farley of Saturday Night Live.

Cocaine and heroin, the fatal Speedball.

Nothing really changes I guess. Just the players.

There is also The Roxbury, and Tattoo and a few others where young hopeful club-goers stand out front hoping the door men will consider them cool enough to be allowed in.

Really sad. A long way from the days when the acts and the club goers hung out in the alley behind The Ashgrove, Bido Lido's or the Whiskey sharing a joint and their lives, together.

I think I forgot to mention The Ashgrove. Sort of a folk bar on Melrose. I first saw The Chambers Brothers and Spirit there. The place burnt down and later became The Improv, another comedy club. The Troubadour was another popular spot at the time, where The Byrds, Joni Mitchell, Bob Dylan, The New Christie Minstrels, Peter, Paul and Mary and the like would play in the early Sixties. It's still in the same place on Santa Monica Blvd.and Doheny. But the bands have changed. John Lennon even managed to get himself thrown out of there with Harry Nilsson one night in the Seventies.

It seems a shame to me that that kind of intimacy has gone out of seeing bands. Back then you were up close and personal in small clubs around town, now the sheer size of the venues detracts somehow from the familiarity of being one with the band, it's ideas and the music. Having to sit so far away you need binoculars and having to have an amplification system that makes it sound like you have your stereo cranked up detracts somehow from hearing a live show. With the big screens and sound you may as well watch it on MTV or VH1.

Except for the experiences of a Beatles or a Who concert, something on that scale, my idea of seeing and hearing an act is in a club where there is communication with whomever is up on stage, where you can see and hear the little nuances and mistakes that accompany a live performance. The Wiltern Theatre is just about the right size. Not sitting up in the gods of some stadium where all you hear is the audiences reaction to music that could just as well be piped in over the amplification system, which it is, but it isn't personal. The popularity is what killed the beast, that and the need for more money as the entourages grew.

I'm sure a lot of the bands from the original bunch sometimes wish they could play some of the clubs again to a small group of loyal friends and followers.

That is probably one reason the MTV *"Un-Plugged"* series of shows have gleaned so much favour and popularity. Well, you had to be there!

It was great, though I wasn't really conscious of all this special stuff going on at the time. We all just sort of took it for the norm, I did anyway. Perhaps that's why it really takes a hell of a lot to impress me nowadays. I haven't really gotten excited about anything new in a long long time. A bit jaded perhaps, or I just expect the ridiculous and absurd along with the phenominal.

Just to go and see the world evolving. From my earliest foray's into social experiences on my own at the Teen Centre's in the Valley, to hanging with the Beatles, to who knows what, I guess I came to expect to be entertained, and entertained well.

There were other unlikely spots for events. Usually just restaurants and coffee shops that were the *'in'* spots for a few weeks, months, or even years.

One of the earliest in my recollection was Canter's Delicatessen on Fairfax. It was standing room only after the clubs every night of the week.

I can recall Phil Spector staying out in his Bentley parked at the curb, with his order to go. One or two of us would pop in and sit for a while, then go back inside and table hop amongst the many booths and tables, even at the counter.

Canter's was open all night, so we had it pretty well occupied during the late night hours till dawn.

Then the move happened. Whether out of our constantly roving spirit or the law moving us all on I don't remember at all. We went to the International House of Pancakes on Sunset, near Hollywood High School for a while. I recall downers were very popular at IHOP then, as were Blueberry pancakes. I think a brief stint at Denny's was in there somewhere as well. Anywhere to congregate.

Then there was always Ben Frank's, which I've already mentioned. I think the change of venues had a lot to do with the management wanting to clear the place of all the hippies every now and then.

I called Heidi's mother, Betty, in Florida not too long ago. I was telling her how some of the people I see on the streets of Hollywood today give me a rather uneasy feeling. Betty shot back that people were scared of us kids back then! So the beat goes on.

I never really thought that Heidi and I were scaring the adults of the Sixties. Weird. I mean we were all for peace and love, totally different form the drive-by shooting and Gangsta stuff prevalent today.

I can see being scared of what you don't know. And the *grown-ups* of our teen years didn't know peace, love, and freedom of expression from a hole in the ground. So obviously we were an unknown element back then, and what you don't know you tend to fear. Whether it seems violent or not it's that fear of the unknown that gets you every time.

I will have to disagree however that Heidi and myself and the rest of us were putting fear into anyone anywhere similar to the unease I feel coming across a group of kids in gang attire hanging around under a freeway bridge at sun-down.

But then again, I should know better than anyone that the old saying of clothes make the man or woman is a fallacy. So the kids dressed like gang members aren't necessarily in gangs. No more than the people who dressed like hippies in the Sixties and Seventies were actually cool.

There was a saying then that you didn't have to have long hair to get high. Lots of guys coming back from the Nam proved that one.

Chapter 17

Now that I have catalogued the L.A. club scene I feel it only fair to go through the London clubs to the best of my ability.

I already have done an extensive overview of The Rainbow, Finsbury Park, and by doing so touched on The Roundhouse. These were actually more concert venues rather than nightclubs, though they had bars.

I reached London in 1969, as I have already chronicled, and after I moved into Cheyne Place with Fiya we started going to The Revolution. This is where I ran into Keith Moon once again.

The Rev, as it was called, was pretty much a nightly occurrence. Then I think it just closed down. I really can't recall, it may have just ceased to be popular. A wide selection of people went there. I used to see Christine Keeler there on occasion. Never saw Mandy Rice Davies though. Fiya, being older was familiar with the characters of the Profumo affair. She would frequent the same places and knew the players quite well.

There were brief visits to places such as Blaises', The Bag of Nails, where Hendrix first played, then there was The Speakeasy. Not so much a club, more a way of life.

The Speak, in Margaret Street, in the West End of London, was down a flight of stairs, in a basement. Upon descending into these nether regions you were greeted with a coffin with a brass plate announcing: "Ashes to ashes, dust to dust, if the women don't get you the whiskey must." This was between the bathrooms.

Then after depositing your coat with Avril in the cloakroom, and greeting Roberto and Mino, you entered the bar area, a horseshoe shaped bar, with gaming machines on the far side, like one-armed bandits, or slot machines as they're called in the States. At the curved end of the bar was the cabaret area with booths down the sides to the dance floor and the stage beyond that. Then to the right, was the restaurant, presided over by Luigi, who later went on to Tramp as the head chef, before going to run the kitchen at J. Arthur's. You could enter the restaurant from the dance floor or the bar area. Now that I'm describing it I remember that as a club it was really laid out well, a very comfortable and unassuming set-up. Though the lower half of the partition around the restaurant was paneled the top half was window, so you could see into the entire restaurant area without going in. Great.

Most of the regular patrons sat in the restaurant, whether we ate or not. Though by 4 am most of us had drunk enough to warrant ordering some scampi, or perhaps one of Luigi's Pepper steaks or steak Tournedos', and oh, his delicious creamed spinach.

At one time Keith speeded up the drink ordering process by bringing in a pair of Walkie-Talkies and placing one behind the bar, saved the waitresses some steps.

Many's the night I was challenged to a drinking match in the restaurant. I drank a lot of grown men under the table there. One night in particular I recall someone called Johnnie Fenton betting he could get me drunk. Said he could never figure out how I could put so much away and never appear drunk. I always held my alcohol very well back then and it exasperated him for some reason. So, we sat in the restaurant with the miniature bottles they served in there increasing on our table as the night wore on. I remember Johnnie slipping slowly under the table before last call was announced, and I? Well, I managed to climb the stairs just fine and hail a cab.

Oh, to have the constitution of a twenty year old again!

Then there was Tramp. I know not from where it sprang, but it was suddenly the place we were at most of the time. It was, until a few years ago, run by Johnnie Gold. He started at the Ad Lib. On a trip to London, before Johnnie retired, both he and the club were still going strong. What was strange is that neither he nor any of his staff had seemed to have aged or changed at all. I asked Guido how this could be, as he took me back in he kitchens to greet Willie, the cook, and some of the other old timers. He said "Johnnie doesn't let us change from 26 years ago!" O.K., I'll buy that!

Tramp has always been the classiest and I suppose the most exclusive of the clubs, but without any pretension. You either fit or you don't. That's probably why it has always been so cool and compatible. In the old days our table usually consisted of Keith and myself, and Dougall, Keith's assistant, and driver, along with Harry Nilsson, Ringo, Billy Laurie (Lulu's brother), the combinations changed, but Keith, Harry and Ringo were the nucleus.

It wasn't all music and show business people. John Conte, the boxer, Georgie Best, the football player were often seen around. On my most recent visit in 1995, Malcolm Allison, the Manchester United manager was in town for the FA Cup Finals and turned up. His team lost to Everton two days later as it so happens. Hope he had a good time!

Tramp in the old days was renowned for it's Prime Rib. Luigi, formally of the Speakeasy, was chef there before going on to J. Arthur's in Parson's Green. Alas, he wasn't there this last time I went, and no one knows where he has moved on to.

This is another short segue. I just mentioned another club I went to regularly for a long, seems like, time. J. Arthur's, in Parson's Green.

A lot of the people from the Speakeasy, after it closed down, ended up here. It was managed, if not actually owned, by John French, the hair stylist. He used to have a place in Bramham Gardens in Earl's Court where I'd go sometimes and hang out with him and my friend David Anthony. In fact this is where I first heard Elton John's first self-titled album. David and John and I had stayed up all night on acid and when it was dawn John put on Elton John's *"Your Song"*. It was a sunny Spring day and we ended up in Regent's Park, I think John Michael joined us. It's when David and John-Michael both had their new Triumph motorcycles. But I digress...

J.Arthur's, as I said was run by John French and had Luigi for the chef. It was basically a supper club, with a dance floor. A rather colourful character, Malcolm Raines was Matri'd of sorts, fondly known as "Percy" he made all welcome. I last saw him in L.A. at the Central, back in the '80's, he was living in Dallas then and just visiting L. A.

There was another guy I knew from J. Arthur's (which in rhyming slang means 'wank' by the way, J. Arthur Rank= Wank)

He was a sweet guy called Dave Cansdale. He was a photographer. He had asthma, he had a big heart, and a shaggy dog called Yogi. Once he took my parents and I on a business trip with him to Paris in a motor home he had. He also had a 1951 Rover which he lent me on occasion.

Unfortunately he also had a fondness for heroin and combined with his asthma, it killed him.

Dave Cansdale and Yogi.

So, enough of this journey, back to Tramp.

Although there is a large disco area with booths and tables all around the dance floor, and I can recall many a night sitting in there with Keith, and usually someone like Dudley Moore or John Conte, it was far too noisy so we would retreat into the restaurant.

Then there was the lounge area with sofa's and a coffee table, this is where you come into when you first descend the stairs. But, the restaurant/bar was, and still is the prime place to hang out when there.

I find myself at a loss for words about Tramp, right now, as I have now revisited it. It warmed my heart that I was so loved and accepted, as though I had never been away. Even though we arrived unannounced, when the place was apparently filled to capacity, with people up at the entrance offering upward of £500 to gain entry. I was immediately recognized and invited to go on in and speak to Johnny about letting Gordon and Chris in. I had to say that Chris was our driver, as they still have the 'escorted men only' rule for most. We had a great, albeit expensive night there, and I shall no doubt elaborate on it more fully when I come to the description of my first trip back in 14 years later on in this narrative.

All indeed to say for now is that it was wonderful stepping back into a world I only remember through a glass darkly and find that my recollections were accurate all along.

What really amazed me was that so many of the staff remembered me so well. Much more so than I could. I may not recall their names, though the faces were all so familiar.

I had always thought, I suppose, that I was sort of an extension of Keith and the people we hung around with, but I was too young to think otherwise. So I was, and now know that I was, always a personage in my own right. It's quite gratifying really. I've made a mark, and no doubt will make more as time goes by. In-other-words, I wasn't just an extension of my companions.

Chapter 18

In the Eighties the obvious occurred and the bands of the Sixties started the phenomenon of the twenty year reunion tour.

I got involved in one of the earliest of these.

I had been over at John Yorks' apartment in Hollywood and Mike Clarke, drummer for the Byrds came by.

John had played with the Byrds when David Crosby left and as the Byrds had now split into two factions, Roger McGuinn and Chris Hillman on one side and Mike Clarke, Gene Clark, Rick Danko, formerly of The Band, a guy called Carlos, and John York starting their own Byrds. I had known Mike way back in the mid-sixties, we started reminiscing, and soon we were hanging out at the house he shared with Gene on Otsego St. in Van Nuys, California.

Drinking beer and doing a bit of blow. We were like high school kids hanging out and going to the Palomino or the Red Lantern I think it was called.

The band got ready and a tour was planned. I joined them in San Francisco. It got too crazy and out of hand, and although fun, the ride back down on the bus from Sacramento, I let Carlos take my car, was strange to say the least. I hung out with Rick Danko, Michael had picked up someone else. Then Carlos disappeared with my car, stranding me at John's for a few days. Then, their manager, Michael Gaiman, who I trusted to bring a goodly sum of money over from England for me with a better exchange rate than the banks were giving, absconded with the whole $10k!

Sex, drugs and rock and roll can be brutal sometimes. Gave me pause and I shied away from that scene very quickly. Never to recoup my money, but I retained my dignity.

Tommy Sommerville, Gene Clark, me and Mike Clarke at the Palomino.

Mike Clarke in San Francisco

Gene Clark, San Francisco

John York & Gene Clark, San Francisco

Another chance meeting was also through a party at John York's. John gave a birthday gathering for our old friend, Mac B. Ray. Bobby Jamison was there and we hit it off. I went to a lot of AA meetings just to run into him over the next few months.

He moved in here with me for a time, when my aunt Adeline still lived here. Going to AA meetings and the movies. Bobby drifted away. As far as I know, no one from my circle of friends has heard of him since.

John York, Marc B. Ray and I

Bobby Jamison at the Central

Chapter 19

Around Christmas 1994, I sent out my usual slew of Christmas cards.

Gordon Waller and his family had always remained on my Christmas card list, as I always received a card from them, albeit written by his wife Gay.

This year, however I got a phone call. From Gordon.

It was quite a surprise as the last time I had spoken to him was when my father had died in 1987. He and my dad were very fond of each other, and I have now come to find out were in touch with each other far more than I knew.

Gordon was asking if I would ever be coming back to visit England. I really, at that time hadn't even considered it. I hadn't been out of the country since I returned here to live in 1981. What with all the animals and such, I thought it would just be impossible.

The next call to come through was from my mother, she also had received a call from Gordon. Someone reaching out?

During the conversation she mentioned that it had been a couple of years since she had seen me and time was passing and all that. She and my aunt Adeline lived together in London, Adeline was not very well. So that, and the fact that Adeline and I clashed on most occasions, well, they hadn't been out for their usual 6 month stays in a couple of years. I said I'd think about it, she said she'd pay for it. Michael Mitchell said he'd pet sit, so the trip was planned.

I made a reservation for the 5th May 1995. The weather being too bad earlier.

I called Gordon back and let him know.

Here began a lot of calls between the time I told him and the time I left for London.

Would I pick him up some boots?, etc. I jokingly said something like "Well, if you feel like it, I need a ride from the airport!" He said "O.K."

Now, he was living some 300 miles away from London, down in Fowey, in Cornwall, so to say he'd come up to pick me up at Heathrow, when we hadn't even seen each other in about 23 years was quite something.

So the day arrived, Michael came down from San Francisco a few days early to get acquainted with all the animals. This is when the puppy Kiowa was still manageable enough, later he would bite just about anyone he came into contact with, so only Karole could pet sit. Michael took me to lunch at Viva, after I went and said my farewells to Sun, my horse, and then Harvey drove us to LAX.

What a culture shock. To arrive back in a city after 14 years absence. Wow!

The flight, all 11 1/2 hours of it, is disorienting enough, let alone all these things that were vaguely familiar coming at me from everywhere.

Gordon and I had arranged to meet in the bar upstairs at Heathrow. I walked in pushing my luggage trolley, looked around and saw some twinkling eyes that reminded me of someone I once knew looking back.

We sat and caught up, only in a round-about fashion, then we headed into London.

The drive was a strange trip in itself, seeing things that were once so familiar, still there, like no time had passed at all. Places I had forgotten about in my conscious mind altogether, right there like I'd never been away. Very dreamlike, especially with a touch of jet lag.

We stopped at a couple of our local pubs. I say our because Gordon once lived in the same area and frequented the Antelope and The Duke of Wellington there in Belgravia. The same pubs that I and my dad went to.

This is one of those revelations I started to mention. When I was living with Keith, Gordon and my father used to meet at these same pubs, Gordon was able to keep track of my doings in those days through my father. Strange to find out after all that time.

We arrived back at my mum's flat in Ebury Street. All the familial stuff needs no explanation, so I won't go into it.

Gordon decided to stay down in London with me for a day or two. I knew not what I was going to do anyway.

I had been on a series of interviews before leaving L.A. for a new record label, FBL. The second day I was in London a fax came through that I had been hired as part of the A&R department at $50,000 a year. This was reason to celebrate. No more trying to make it in films, doing stunt work, stand-in work and background actor (extra) work.

We went here and there. Gordon decided I should come down to Cornwall with him and meet his family.

So, we went. I was only over for a fortnight (two weeks), and there was a rush on everything.

The drive was lovely. The countryside appealing to me much more than the sprawling, dirty and crowded city of London that had attracted me so in my younger days.

Gordon's wife, Gay, an Australian woman was courteous but cautious. His daughter Phillippa was sweet, only 15, another Capricorn, and his other, older daughter, Natalie, was as guarded as her mother.

Phillipa, Gay and I in Fowey, Cornwall, May 1995.

Gordon showed me all around the Cornish countryside, and Fowey, it was fun. One evening, while drinking at the Fowey Hotel he decided to take me out on his boat and went to get it while Gay, Philly and I went back to the house to change. I guess I had had too much hard cider, for coming down the spiral, hanging staircase I slipped and landed on a bolt sticking out of the stair, puncturing my thigh.

Gordon came to the surgery and took me to Truro to the hospital there as the local doctor couldn't do what needed to be done in his office.

They shot my leg full of a local anesthetic and probed around cleaning it out and stitched me up. I needed to stay in hospital overnight so they could drain the wound and do all that stuff.

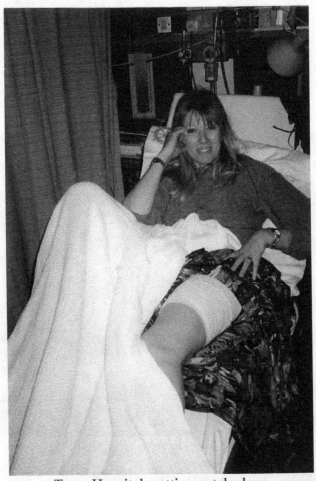

Truro Hospital, getting patched up.

In the back of my mind I had always sort of feared going back to England. I think after that nightmare of the accident I'd had in 1978, I thought I might get trapped over there again, and here I was in hospital!

Gordon came and picked me up the next day. I called the airlines to extend my stay an extra 4 days, as I couldn't fly right away, not with new sutures. After deciding to go back to London on the train, Gordon decided he couldn't let me hobble all over on trains and he drove me up. This is where his friend, though I hesitate to call him that now, came into the picture.(He later turned out to be a thief.)

Chris, his friend, wanted to get to London and would share the driving and petrol expenses.

We took off and got to London that evening and cleaned up to go to dinner, we had a great Chinese meal and then decided to go to a club.

All the places I had known were gone, or changed. Prissy doormen refusing to let non-members in etc. So off to Jermyn Street and Tramp.

Chapter 20

This is where I came in. Or rather came back, and have already explained the feelings on returning that night, the friendliness and acceptance. It was great. But although all the staff was there and the same, the new clientèle were all strangers, so *that* one little thing was missing. No Ringo, no Keith, no Harry, no...anyone we knew. Just Johnny and Jackie Collins, and they're part of the staff really.

I returned to L.A. toward the end of May, and the phone calls started.

Gordon, I had figured from spending these past couple of weeks with him, was not a happy camper. He seemed sort of in limbo about everything, and not really very well-balanced. He was depressed and he was drinking too much. All the usual red flags.

He had re-formed an attachment to me over those two weeks, and was obviously in love, or heading that way fast.

So we talked a lot. I was still waiting to get working with this new FBL record label. Gordon was restless and depressed. I suggested he come out to L.A. for a visit. He hadn't been out here in 20 years, why not.

So I made reservations and he arrived 15th September 1995. After the jet lag, which affects him more than I, and all the nervousness and accompanying stuff was gotten over, he actually started to perk up. We visited old friends of his and of mine, he was recognized when we went out and made to realize his life in show business wasn't finished. All in all a lot of good was done.

Then he returned to the U.K. and the bad set in again. I went over for Christmas that year, it was so cold. I stayed three weeks that time, and everything was better, until he returned to Cornwall for Christmas Day, then on Boxing Day we re-grouped again at his sister Anne's and her fiancée Charles in Crawley. All in all it was becoming apparent to me that home was not where his heart was. In fact it seemed to be lacking in everything good for him. I returned to L.A.

I think Gordon came out in January that time. We had inadvertently fallen in love with each other. Gordon just needed to get over some problems and obstacles. His marriage was definitely over, years before actually, so there was nothing left to do but announce it .Oh, there were arguments and accusations and all the encumbering baggage that goes with ending something that died years ago anyway.

I had come in contact with a producer who needed a soundtrack for a film he was doing about James Dean, and while Gordon was still in England had told him about it.
He wrote a couple of songs relating to the synopsis, in about 15 minutes I might add, and so the beginning of Steel Wallet International, Ltd., a publishing company, had it's first assignment.
I went over again, ostensibly to see the Who perform *Quadrophenia* in Hyde Park in June 1996. Gordon and I went together. It was great. the Who, Eric Clapton, Bob Dylan and Alanis Morrisette.

Gordon and I are always teasing each other about who we have been involved with, even if only for one night. We were in The Duke before going off to Hyde Park and he said something about were there any others, that we might see today, that he should know about. I mentioned that once, when I was arguing with Keith or something, that well, Roger had called and invited me down to Burwash to visit. I went and, well it was a long time ago, and no romance, just good friends, it is something that happens a lot I think. So he jokingly said "Oh, I see, any more...?" and on it went. Later, when we were waiting at the enclosure for our passes I saw Heather, Roger's wife, and said hello. Heather kept staring over my shoulder, so I asked if she knew Gordon Waller. With that she ran over and threw herself in his arms. Seems that way back in 1964, while a dancer on the same Murray the K shows Peter & Gordon were playing, well they were an item. Touché!
This time Gordon and I flew back to L.A. together.
Things were getting better on all fronts. As I previously said, we had started a publishing company when the whole deal with that record label turned out to be a con worked on the investors of this bogus company. The fake CEO went to jail. I made a friend in Rox, another 'employee', and that was all that came of that.
Though the film *"James Dean-Race With Destiny"* didn't get properly released nor circulated in the States, the CD Gordon wrote

produced and performed is great. We needed a label to put it out, and we needed the film to be released for that. It still gains high praise from those who have heard it. It is available if you look.

This is where the re-entry in my life and my living room came with Keith Allison writing a song or two with Gordon for the album.

What comes around surely goes around.

So, the chronology of events so far, in brief, are, Gordon went back January of 1997 for a short time, his trips over there have never been good for his health, we need to be together, even then the U.K. triggers some bad stuff in him. Then we were here in L.A. again. We traveled from San Diego up to San Francisco in June, the Summer of Love's 30th anniversary. I touched on all this earlier. Going through the past to the present, Big Sur and Sausalito, all the places I traveled in the 60s as hippies, staying at Michael Mitchell's place in San Francisco and driving back. It was a lovely trip. Cleansing.

Then Gordon returned to England in August, I had my ticket already for September 8th, this would have me there for his mother, Elizabeth's, birthday and my mother's birthday at the end of the month, on the 26th.

Off I went again, at least had some good weather this time.

I arrived three days after the funeral of Princess Diana, there were wilting flowers everywhere. Gordon took me to Westminster Abbey, where the funeral had been. He had gone to school at Westminster, so he knew it all very well.

I returned on the 29th of September and Gordon came back the 14th October.

Gordon had been back in England for almost three weeks. He was doing well till he saw his wife on her way to Australia, something set him off. Doesn't take much I have come to find.

Their divorce was almost final, Gordon came back in March for six months. We had spoken about marriage, it was in the cards.

The whole thing came right and not the way I originally had thought the plans would go.

But it was better.

March arrived and Gordon returned, still up in the air about many decisions in his life, and in mine.

My how time flies. We have had the good times and the not-so-good. But here it is. A new century and since I last wrote in this journal of sorts so much has transpired.

So when I last wrote Gordon came back in March. That was 1998.

His divorce papers, the Final Decree, came through one July day and we drove up to Ventura and got a marriage license. Then Gordon went off to Texas to play with Denny Laine and Scott Moss in Ft. Worth at a few clubs. I had been in England and flew back, came home, re-packed, changed and went to Burbank airport and onto Dallas/Ft. Worth. It was very hot there, too hot for people to come out. Really, a pity, as the shows were great.

We had planned to marry at the beach, as Gordon said we had, after all, met there, how romantic. But the beach was all churned up thanks to the rains of El Nino.

We got back and found Kathy Holland had decided we should marry at her and Terry's house in Simi Valley. So we decided on the 15th August 1998 and went for it.

Trying to organize a wedding in only a few weeks was quite something. Kathy did well. Too bad she turned out to not be the friend to me I thought she was. But as they say, that's show business, (and the people who are on the fringes of it, moving in, getting pushy and rising above their station in other's lives.)

Chapter 21

I had gone to Shepler's in Arlington, Texas and found a wedding dress. We stopped at a flea market and got silver rings. We were set.

I must say, Kathy did us proud and after I gave her a list of friends and their numbers she organized it well in spite of us, even if she ended up assuming all those people as *her* friends!

She even managed to throw a Bridal Shower for me and I got lots of lovely lingerie. The day approached and Gordon got his tux and I suggested he ask Peter Asher to be his best man. I got my old friend Gail Murphy as Matron of Honour and the day arrived. I was planning on getting ready at Kathys' salon, so went up the 118 freeway and got there to find I had forgotten my going-away stuff and make-up. So a quick drive back and up again. Well, they couldn't start without me.

Gail and Mick Schnieder came to the salon and I was ready and got driven to the house. We have video footage of everything from the moment we drove up, We arrived separately, as Gordon had spent the night in Malibu at Peter's. Obeying tradition as-it-were.

Star taped it all and the entertainment was phenomenal. Peter and Gordon played together for the first time in 29 years, I must say I asked for Peter and Gordon to sing *"Woman"* for me. I had always considered it my song as Gordon had first played it to my parents and I in Benedict Canyon, as "A song Paul wrote that we just recorded" was how Gordon introduced it. Today, they have gotten back together, after 37 years this time, for a benefit concert for Mike Smith of the Dave Clark Five. But I get way ahead of myself.

The party went on and on. Spencer Davis, Dave Perlman, Tom MacLear, Jim Blazer, Chris Montez, Jovan and a host of others jammed all night. Gordon's sister, Anne and fiancée, Charles flew over from England and surprised Gordon. A lot of old friends were there. It was a great wedding.

Wedding Day: Gail Murphy, Gordon and I and Peter Asher
15th August 1998.

Dave Perlman, Gordon, Spencer Davis and Terry Reid.

We had been given a night at the Four Season's in Santa Barbara by Peter and went off the next day after and bit of re-organization. The party was so good we couldn't leave, and Karole got too drunk and wandered off so we had to make sure Gulliver and Kiowa and all the birds were taken care of.

So, married at last. Never thought I would do it actually. What a trip.

What a trip indeed. A strange one, getting things right took a while. Now almost 8 years later we have had falling outs and re established friendships with friends and family. Some have now departed. Adeline, my aunt, died two days before our wedding. My mother was happy to see me married I am sure. We went over to London and got married all over again for our families on the 16th September at St. Mary's, Bourne Street.

We had a party, thrown by my mother at the Cavalry Club in Piccadilly. David Anthony, David Brown, Philip and Penny Townsend showed to this one, L.A. was too far to come for the first I suppose.

We had a "second" honeymoon at the white Horse Inn in Rickmansworth courtesy of David Brown and his lady at the time. This after a rousing send off at the Duke of Wellington in Belgravia. Courtesy of the great landlord John Bond. What a crazy tube ride in wedding clothes that was!

16th September 1998. London wedding with "the families".

GEORGIANA STEELE-WALLER

Chapter 22

My arthritis kept getting worse, my walking was painful, riding near impossible. Finally, in August of 2004, I relented and got my right hip replaced. It was wonderful. No more pain. So good that I had the left one done six months later in March of 2005.   In the summer of 2006 I had been back in the saddle, properly, pain free for a year. It is miraculous. In fact my surgeon, Dr. Miric is a miracle worker.

I mentioned this benefit for Mike Smith. He had a bad accident about four years ago and broke his neck. He is paralyzed from the chest down and needs certain things.

Paul Shaffer, from the David Letterman show, called Peter, who called Gordon and the reunion, for one night only, was set up.

It was held at B. B.Kings in New York City, 2nd August 2004.

It was a rousing success. Denny Laine, Billy J. Kramer, the Zombies, and the Fab Faux played two shows into the wee hours and it was wonderful.

Peter and Gordon
BB KINGS   NEW YORK

Peter and Gordon at B.B. Kings benefit for Mike Smith, August 2005.

Since that night the offers have been rolling in and Peter & Gordon are together again.

They are doing a few gigs a month. Have already been to the Philippines and a few cities in the US., Canada and the Far East are in the works and things are good there.

Gordon just celebrated his 61st birthday and Peter, 62 a few weeks later. Still younger than McCartney or any of the Stones, so many good touring years left, we hope!

Chapter 23

With the good comes the sorrowful.

In September of 2005, my mother, at 94 decided to come and visit. She arrived the 30th and was not herself, I put it down to her age and the long trip. She lingered around for a couple of weeks and then, I realized she had been keeping falls and such from me. I called for an ambulance and she got to hospital. She was really bad. Then she rallied. She had had a stroke and the doctors were all amazed at her quick rebounding recovery. Then On the 15 October the Doctor phoned to say she had aspirated some food and it didn't look good. That call was followed shortly thereafter with the dreaded one. Mum passed away October 15th at about 1:20 in the afternoon. I didn't even have time to get there. She looked so pretty and peaceful when I did go. It is still unbelievable. But she did have a 'do not resuscitate' order.

Gordon had just returned from England in time to see her. I recall the first thing she asked him was how was her beautiful great-granddaughter. Natalie had a baby girl, Tyla, four years before. One day after my mum's 90th birthday. Then began the final arrangements. I was trying to manage here with the organizing of her flat and things in London, not knowing how to do it all.

Howard, the companion she had taken in, told me not to worry, he had promised her he would pack everything up for me and arrange sales at auction houses.

Oh yes. He certainly played her, and me. As it turned out Mr Howard Mutte-Mewse packed up all the family silver, lace, crystal and jewelry and took it to Christie's auction house in London and put it all up for auction, under his name. I have lost everything. I have legal action pending, to what good I do not know at this writing.

Have to be practical and hope for the best.

144

Howard Mutte-Mewse, mum, Johanna & Austin Mutte-Mewse

Had to get back to real life too.
Karma is a bitch and things will take care to come right, I hope.

Peter & Gordon continued touring throughout the Spring and Summer of 2006. There was Akron, San Diego, Vegas and Toronto.

There were plans, with Nancy Bragin in Philidelphia, for a DVD and CD of a live shows in Toronto. Talk of a book deal too. Then something happened. The drinking began again, with a vengeance.

Gordon couldn't be stopped. It actually began before the Toronto gigs in October. Ray came down from San Francisco to help sober him up for those, but by the 9th, when they came back, Gordon was at it again. I have to go about my day-to-day, it pained me deeply to see him go downhill like this, especially when things were going so well..

Before the Toronto shows Gordon was raging drunk when I came home from riding one night. Ray was here with him, in the kitchen, and Gordon took me by the hand and led me to our room. He was crying and upset, said he had met someone.

My God! What did he mean? Surely he was joking? He said she was someone he met when he was 18 and she came to the Vegas show in September.

When he sobered up I asked him about it and he sloughed it off as being a made up story.

So, things were good again for a while.

Meanwhile, Peter Asher was going to be guest of honour at their old school, Westminster. He thought it would be fun, at the end of the speech to bring Gordon out and sing a song or two. He made all the plans and travel arrangements. The time was now drawing near for Gordon to join him in London. Gordon drank more and more. Ray, once again came down from San Francisco .I was laid up with back problems. This time Gordon was reeling. It was the weekend of the Who concert at the Hollywood Bowl, I, of course had my passes and so forth. Gordon didn't want to go. Michael Mitchell came down from San Francisco, so along with Ray, and then Karole we had a full house.

Gordon was getting more and more belligerent and nasty and Ray could not even prevent him from getting more liquor. On the day Gordon was to leave we all had a hell of a time trying to get him sober enough to shower, packed and so forth. He was adamant that he was OK. Ray found another bottle of Southern Comfort and poured it out.

Gordon got behind the wheel of his car and, as Ray was leaning in the window trying to stop him, Gordon floored it, throwing Ray across the road and fracturing his pelvis and elbow.

Gordon with Ray Denman, November 2005

This was really bad, he was mean and nasty and no one could really believe the things coming out of his mouth. This wasn't my Gordon. It is truly terrible what alcohol does to some people. Of course it is a disease. I find it makes people harder to handle than any drugs known to man.

I had been laid up since the end of October with terrible sciatica. The epidural I received on Halloween did little to relieve it this time. I couldn't handle all that was going on as well.

The car came for Gordon and we all managed to get him off to meet Peter. It was touch and go for a while whether Gordon would even be allowed on the flight, unfortunately he was. I say that because of the events that followed.

Needless to say, Gordon walked out on Peter, his night, his honour, his embarrassment.

Peter then announced he would never sing with Gordon again. So for the second time Gordon's drinking broke up the duo. The first being in about 1968. Very sad.

Then Gordon, though Peter had arranged a flight for him back to L.A., disappeared. No one knew his whereabouts till he phoned someone, said he was in Atlanta. He never phoned me and apparently had purchased a pay-as-you-go phone before all this happened. More and more curious.

I have been agonizing over whether to write about this segment of our lives, but as it is my journal, of sorts, and I am being truthful and factual, what is the harm. It is the truth, no matter how sad.

Like I said in an earlier chapter, if you are ashamed of anything in your past, you probably shouldn't have done it to begin with.

Gordon finally turned up at this woman's apartment in New York City.

He wouldn't take my calls, nor anyone else's. I, of course, was afraid at first and got talked into taking out a restraining order, so he wouldn't call or show up unexpectedly.

Now, some months later, he is starting to come out of his shell. He went to see Peter and they hashed out a plan to continue playing gigs together.

He started phoning me the other day and is civil, but confused as to his plans. He knows he needs to move on and is afraid to come home. I pray daily this will change and he will return and we can make everything even better than it was before. I am sure all couples reading this will know what I mean when I say we became complacent, too used to each other, took each other for granted. I know I have grown from this separation and I hope he has as well. There is no romance, he says, between him and this woman. I want so to believe it. He came to collect his things, but not to put in a home, just in storage. He can always bring them back. He obviously has pressure from family and people such as Kathy Holland, to keep away from me, I know he can't have fallen out of love with me completely, but he is damaged.

So, as I wind this down till another time, I live in hope that my husband of eight years, my love of 41 years, will realize where he belongs and come home. We will both have to change if this is to happen. I realize as time passes it was not a healthy relationship as it was. I pray that he will try to do right by himself and others. We all deserve another chance. Thanks for listening. This long strange trip is definitely not over yet.

Maybe we can talk again sometime.

THE END

Photo Gallery

Robert Mitchum & I on set.

Willie Nelson & I

Sam Elliot & I, set of Roadhouse.

Ami Albea, Mickey Dolenz & I on Mickey's birthday.

Harvey Gardner, Willie Nelson, Iron Eyes Cody & I.

Gordon, Mel Carter & I in Tucson.

Ben Gazzara, me and Eva Marie Saint, set of "People Like Us".

Gordon & I with Alan Phillips on his 50th.

Mark Hudson & I, Chicago

Trigger and I and some of the Triggerette Bluebirds.

Peter Noone (Herman), me and Gordon, San Diego.

Keith Allison and I

Gordon & I with Ronnie Frazier and Kim Gardner (Ashton, Gardner & Dyke), London.

Tony Ashton & I, London.